THE LITTLE
BLACK BOOK OF

WASHINGTON, DC

CONTENTS

INTRODUCTION

A city of living history, Washington, DC is home to the U.S. President and Congress, the capital of the largest democratic nation in the world, and the only city established by the U.S. Constitution. But Washington is more than that. It is one of the most vibrant, diverse, and beautiful cities in the U.S. and the world. Dotted with parks and plazas, monuments and memorials, Washington, DC takes its name from two places: "Washington" from President Washington, and "District of Columbia" from a poetic name for the U.S. popular at that time. Based on the vision of French engineer turned American soldier Pierre Charles L'Enfant, Washington boasts all the beauty of a European city—diagonal boulevards, parks and gardens, and the grandeur of giant but not towering edifices.

Because no building is more than 20 feet taller than the width of the street or avenue it faces, light pours into the capital city, creating a bright, exciting backdrop for momentous decisions and daily life. More than five million people live and work in the DC region.

Washington is not part of any state, but, at first, was a diamond-shaped city—100 square miles—carved from parts of Maryland and Virginia. In 1846, Congress returned some 30 square miles to Virginia. Beyond the city limits lies the Beltway, Interstate 495, a roadway that encircles Washington's closest suburbs in Maryland and Virginia. Situated midway along the East Coast, it is 90 miles inland from the Atlantic Ocean and 233 miles south of New York City. It's comprised of four quadrants—NW, SW, NE, and SE—that meet at the U.S. Capitol.

Washington is a city built on compromise. In the beginning, Thomas Jefferson and the Southern states sought to situate the new capital city near the southern agricultural region. Alexander Hamilton and the Northern states wanted the new nation to absorb Revolutionary War debt. In the end, both got what they wanted.

George Washington chose the spot for the new capital on the northern bank of the Potomac River, not far from his Virginia home across the river at Mount Vernon.

The "horse trading" that characterizes the city's origins continues today on Capitol Hill. When disagreements arise, debates erupt, filibusters ensue, and deals are struck.

Washington is two cities. The first is the official city and seat of the federal government that includes the White House and departments of the executive branch; the U.S. Capitol where the House and Senate meet; and the U.S. Supreme Court, the highest court in the land. The other is the city of neighborhoods and suburbs where many federal workers live and play.

Washington, DC, or simply DC, is a bargain compared to other big city destinations. Most of DC's major attractions—including National Park monuments, touring federal buildings, and the Smithsonian Museums—are free. DC's neighborhoods offer many free concerts and outdoor festivals. And be sure to indulge in the city's food scene, where you'll find traditional power dining rooms, stylish restaurants, and every type of ethnic eatery.

GETTING AROUND WASHINGTON

Washington is a relatively easy place to navigate. Visitors can choose from a variety of forms of transportation to reach every area of the city, as well as the Virginia and Maryland suburbs.

Washingtonians tend to be well-informed people, so whether you are using the Metro, Metrobus, or DC Circulator bus, ask questions when traveling. You won't be disappointed. Remember, this is a government town where information is the main industry. Pick up a Metro map at any Metro stop. You also can find Metrobus maps for routes that connect to that Metro station there.

The Washington Metropolitan Area Transit Authority (WMATA) *(www.wmata.com)* operates the subway lines and bus routes throughout the DC area. The Metrorail system, or simply the Metro, opened in 1976, helping to transform the nation's capital into an international center. What began as the Red Line, running from the Metro Center in downtown Washington in a U-shape to the Maryland suburbs, has spread out into an extensive network of underground rail transportation on the Blue, Orange, Yellow, and Green Lines. The Washington Metro is arguably the cleanest, quietest underground rail system in the world. If your hotel is situated near a Metro stop, by all means hop on the Metro and ride to your destination. Purchase a SmarTrip for travel on both the Metro and Metrobus. Fares depend on the distance traveled and the time of day, with a surcharge added during morning and evening weekday rush hours. And be sure to get your own SmarTrip card; fare cards can't be shared. Fares are subtracted automatically. Regular and SmarTrip fare cards can be purchased at Metro rail stations throughout the city, and fares are deducted from the card upon exiting. (Which means hang on to your fare card—you will need it to exit at your destination!) Route maps are posted at every station and inside each Metro car. Each train displays the name of its final destination. *(See the Metro map at the end of this book.)*

A warning regarding mass transit: Washington is not a 24-hour city. The Metro opens at 5AM weekdays and 7AM weekends, but shuts down at midnight Sunday–Thursday. It stays open until 3AM Friday and Saturday.

The Metro operates most everywhere a visitor is likely to go, with the exception of Georgetown and Adams-Morgan, which are accessible only by car and bus. If you are in less of a hurry and want to see the sights while you travel, try the Metrobus, or pick up one of the DC Circulator *(www.dccirculator.com)* buses for just a dollar. You can pay with exact change or with a SmarTrip card. It has six routes throughout the city. The Georgetown-Union Station route is especially popular with visitors.

Schedules for the Metrobus system vary from bus to bus. Transfer from the Metro to a bus using a SmarTrip card and you will pay a reduced fare. Contact 202-637-7000 or visit www.wmata.com to check information for either the Metro or Metrobus.

GETTING TO WASHINGTON

Three airports serve the city: Ronald Reagan National Airport, Dulles International Airport, and Baltimore/ Washington International Airport. Ronald Reagan Washington National Airport (DCA), referred to as National Airport *(703-417-8000, www.mwaa.com/ reagan)*, is situated south of the city along the Potomac River, just 15 minutes from downtown and Capitol Hill. If you are planning to stay downtown, in Georgetown, or even in Upper Northwest, it's the most convenient way to arrive. Domestic flights on major, regional, and commuter airlines fly into National, and it affords easy access to the city's Metro Blue and Yellow Lines.

Dulles International Airport (IAD) *(703-572-2700, www.mwaa.com/dulles)* is located in Virginia, 26 miles west of the city. A variety of domestic and international carriers fly into Dulles. To get into the city, take the Washington Flyer Coach *(703-685-1400, 888-washfly, www.washfly.com)* to the West Falls Church Metro station (Orange Line); it leaves every 30 minutes.

Baltimore/Washington International Thurgood Marshall Airport (BWI) *(410-859-7100, www.bwiairport.com)* is another option, located 30 miles from Washington. Both domestic and international flights arrive here, but taxi fare to the city can be high. The MARC train (weekdays only) and Amtrak serve BWI Rail Station, from which free shuttles take you to the airport terminal. BWI Express Metrobus runs between BWI and the Greenbelt Metro station (Green Line) every 40 minutes. SuperShuttle *(202-296-6662, 800-BLUEVAN, www.supershuttle.com)* offers door-to-door shared ride van service from each of the three DC area airports. Another option, of course, is to rent a car.

If you're arriving from New York City, Amtrak *(800-USARAIL, www.amtrak.com)* runs intercity and high-speed trains between New York's Penn Station and Washington's Union Station. New York to DC is an increasingly popular bus run. Boltbus *(www.boltbus.com)*, Megabus *(www.megabus.com)*, Washington Deluxe *(866-287-6932, www.washny.com)*, and other bus lines all offer inexpensive service between the two cities.

CITY TOURS

City Segway Tours of Washington, DC offers 3-hour guided tours of the city on the Segway Personal Transporter. Tours leave daily at 10AM, 2PM, and 6PM from downtown DC, and cost $70 per person. *(624 9th St. NW, 1-877-Seg-Tour, www.citysegwaytours.com/washington-dc)*

Tourmobile Sightseeing is a National Park Service concession offering hop-on/hop-off narrated bus/tram "American Heritage" tours of DC's major sights, including Arlington Cemetery, as well as an Arlington Cemetery-only tour. They also offer seasonal bus tours to Mount Vernon. *(888-868-7707 or 202-554-5100, www.tourmobile.com)*

Bike and Roll offers professionally guided bike tours of the monuments or historic capital sites (adults $40/kids 12 and under $30), plus two different night tours (adults $45/kids $35). *(202-842-BIKE, www.bikeand roll.com)*

DC Metro Food Tours present walking culinary tours of DC's neighborhoods and are a great way to combine history, sightseeing, and eating. *(202-683-8847, www.dcfoodtours.com)*

Old Town Trolley Tours operates a fleet of green and orange trolleys which allow reboarding at 19 locations throughout the District. Friendly drivers provide informative and fun commentary. They also offer a nightly Monuments by Moonlight tour. *(202-832-9800, www.trolleytours.com)*

Capitol River Cruises has tours of the Potomac River that depart from Georgetown. Getting out on the water is the best part of taking this affordable, 45-minute narrated cruise. *(301-460-7447, www.capitolrivercruises.com)*

DC by Foot offers free, one-mile walking tours of the monuments, including twilight tours in the spring and summer. Meet at the corner of 15th and Constitution NW next to the Department of Commerce. Guides wear light blue shirts. Tips are appreciated! *(202-370-1830, www.dcbyfoot.com)*

OnBoard Tours offers DC The Best! Tour, which combines a bus tour with short guided walks to get close up and explore DC's attractions with greater depth. It leaves daily at 10:30AM and 2:30PM from the Old Post Office *(12th St. and Pennsylvania Ave.) (301-839-5261 or 877-U-TOUR-DC, www.onboarddctours.com)*

DC Ducks drives by all the monuments, and then plunges into the Potomac for a scenic cruise. Leaves from Union Station *(50 Massachusetts Ave.)* hourly for a 90-minute tour. *(800-213-2474, www.dcducks.com)*

On Location Tours visits over 30 DC TV and movie sites, such as the bar used in *St. Elmo's Fire* and the house used in *The Exorcist*. Tours leave Saturdays at 10AM near Union Station and last about two and a half hours. *(212-209-3370 or 800-979-3370, www.screentours.com)*

HOW TO USE THIS GUIDE

We have included a fold-out map with each chapter to provide a neighborhood by neighborhood guide to the city. Color-coded keys help you find on the maps the places mentioned in the text. **Red** symbols indicate **Places to See**, including landmarks, arts and entertainment, and activities for children. **Blue** symbols indicate **Places to Eat & Drink**, which include restaurants, cafés, and nightspots. **Orange** symbols indicate **Where to Shop**. Finally, **Green** symbols show **Where to Stay**.

Below are our keys for restaurant and hotel prices:

Restaurants
Price of an appetizer and main course without drinks
($) Up to $25
($$) $25 to $45
($$$) $45 and up

Hotels
Price per night
($) $50 to $125
($$) $125 to $250
($$$) $250 and up

MORE TIPS FOR VISITORS

Destination DC *(901 7th St. NW, 4th fl., 202-789-7000 or 800-422-8644, www.destinationdc.org or www.washington.org)* is a comprehensive information source for visitors. Contact them for up-to-the-minute hotel availability. The **DC Visitor Information Center**, run by the Chamber of Commerce, *(1300 Pennsylvania Ave. NW, in the Ronald Reagan Building, www.DCChamber.org)* is another good source of visitor information. Want to catch a show while you're in town? **TicketPlace** *(407 7th St. NW, bet. D and E Sts. www.ticketplace.org)* sells half-price, day-of, and advance tickets. Tickets can be bought in person or online. Credit or debit card only, no cash or checks.

SEASONAL EVENTS

Winter

National Christmas Tree Lighting Ceremony.

(Early December) The president and his family welcome the season and flip the switch to light the National Christmas Tree. National acts provide entertainment. *(Ellipse south of the White House; tickets required for every attendee, including children; the National Park Service distributes free tickets via an online lottery at www.thenationaltree.org in early November.)*

Illumination of the National Christmas Tree and Pathway of Peace. (Nightly, dusk–11PM from the date of the National Tree Lighting–January 1) 56 small trees representing the 50 states, five territories, and the District of Columbia—the Pathway of Peace—surround the National Christmas Tree. Other seasonal displays include a Yule log, large-scale model train, and manger scene. Musical entertainment each evening by volunteer choirs and bands. *(Ellipse south of the White House, 202-208-1631, www.thenationaltree.org)*

Lighting of the National Menorah. (December) Lighting of the world's largest menorah to mark the eight-day festival of Hanukkah. Musical performances, and latkes

and donuts for all. *(northwest end of the Ellipse near Constitution Ave., tickets required for reserved seating, standing room available without tickets, 202-332-5600, www.nationalmenorah.org)*

15

Spring

National Cherry Blossom Festival. (Late March–early April) a celebration of spring and the 1912 gift of 3,000 pink-and-white blossoming cherry trees from the city of Tokyo. Highlights include the National Cherry Blossom Festival Parade and the Blossom Kite Festival on the grounds of the Washington Monument. *(Tidal Basin surrounding Jefferson Memorial and city-wide, 877-44BLOOM, www.nationalcherryblossomfestival.org)*

St. Patrick's Day Parade. (On the Sunday closest to St. Patrick's Day) Step dancers, floats, marching bands, and bagpipers parade down Constitution Avenue. *(www.dcstpatsparade.com)*

White House Easter Egg Roll. (First Monday after Easter) Fun for children ages 12 and under and their families. *(White House South Lawn; tickets required; the White House distributes free tickets via online lottery in late winter, 202-456-7041, www.whitehouse.gov/eastereggroll)*

Passport DC. (Month of May) DC Embassies open their doors to the general public with displays and demonstrations of the music, dance, crafts, and cuisine of their nations. *(www.passportdc.org)*

National Memorial Day Parade. Memorial Day, free event honoring U.S. veterans with marching military units (active and retired), bands and parade floats. *(703-302-1012, www.nationalmemorialdayparade.com)*

Summer:

DC Jazz Festival. (Early-mid June) An almost two-week international jazz festival with free concerts staged on the National Mall and at venues throughout DC. *(202-457-7625, www.dcjazzfestival.org)*

Capital Pride. (June) Fourth largest gay pride event in the U.S.; includes live entertainment, parade, and street festival. *(202-719-5304, www.capitalpride.org)*

Independence Day. (July 4) A noontime National Parade along Constitution Ave., an evening concert by the National Symphony, and one of the country's largest fireworks displays. *(202-747-3467, www.july4thparade.com or www.nps.gov/foju)*

The Smithsonian Folklife Festival. (July) Celebration of international living traditions with day and evening programs of music, song, dance, crafts, cooking, storytelling, and more. *(National Mall, 202-633-6440, www.festival.si.edu)*

Twilight Tattoo. (Select Wednesdays in May and June) Sunset military pageant performed by members of the 3rd U.S. Infantry (The Old Guard), the U.S. Army Band "Pershing's Own," the Fife and Drum Corps, and the U.S. Army Drill Team; bleacher seating on a first-come, first-served basis. *(Fort McNair, 4th St. and Maine Ave., SW, 202-685-2888, www.twilight.mdw.army.mill/)*

Screen on the Green. (Monday evenings in July and August) Bring a blanket to watch classic films on a giant screen, beginning around 8:30PM. *(National Mall bet. 4th and 7th Streets, 877-262-5866)*

Autumn:

Black Family Reunion Celebration. (September) Celebration of the African-American family; features live music, traditional foods, and arts and crafts. *(National Mall; reunion is free; opening ceremony and prayer breakfast tickets can be purchased by calling 202-737-0120, www.ncnw.org/events/reunion)*

Adams Morgan Day. (2nd Sunday in September) Popular DC festival fetes the international character and famous murals of the Adams Morgan neighborhood; live music, international food, colorful vendors, cultural demonstrations, and kids' fair. *(202-232-1960, www.adamsmorgandayfestival.com)*

National Book Festival. (September) Free festival features authors, illustrators, and poets; sponsored by the Library of Congress. *(National Mall, 888-714-4696, www.loc.gov/bookfest)*

Veterans Day. (November 11) U.S. veterans are honored with wreath-laying ceremonies, speeches, storytelling, and other commemorations at memorials throughout Washington, including Arlington National Cemetery, the African-American Civil War Memorial, the U.S. Navy Memorial, and the Vietnam Veterans Memorial. *(202-619-7222, www.nps.gov/ncro)*

WASHINGTON, DC'S TOP PICKS

Washington offers an abundance of one-of-a-kind attractions and experiences not to be missed! Here's a sampling:

chapter 1

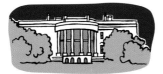

THE WHITE HOUSE AND
THE MONUMENTS

LAFAYETTE SQUARE
AND ENVIRONS

THE WHITE HOUSE AND
THE MONUMENTS
LAFAYETTE SQUARE
AND ENVIRONS

Places to See:

1. WHITE HOUSE ★
2. White House Visitor Center
3. Dwight D. Eisenhower Executive Office Building
4. U.S. Treasury Building
5. President's Park and the Ellipse
6. WASHINGTON MONUMENT ★
7. NATIONAL WORLD WAR II MEMORIAL ★
8. Constitution Gardens
9. VIETNAM VETERANS MEMORIAL ★
10. LINCOLN MEMORIAL ★
11. Korean War Veterans Memorial
12. Tidal Basin
13. DC World War I Memorial
14. Martin Luther King National Memorial
15. Franklin Delano Roosevelt Memorial
16. THOMAS JEFFERSON MEMORIAL ★
17. U.S. HOLOCAUST MEMORIAL MUSEUM ★
18. Bureau of Engraving and Printing
19. National Aquarium
36. St. John's Episcopal Church
37. Equestrian Statue of President Andrew Jackson
38. Statue of Lafayette
39. Blair House
40. Decatur House
41. Octagon House
42. Renwick Gallery of the Smithsonian American Art Museum
43. Corcoran Gallery of Art
44. American Red Cross Visitors Center
45. Daughters of the American Revolution Museum
46. DAR Constitution Hall
47. Art Museum of the Americas

★ *Top Pick*

Places to Eat & Drink:

Where to Shop:

Where to Stay:

How prophetic L'Enfant was when he laid out Washington as a city that goes around in circles!

—*John Mason Brown*

THE WHITE HOUSE AND THE MONUMENTS

 to Foggy Bottom-GWU, or Farragut West, or McPherson Square, or Metro Center, or Federal Triangle, or Smithsonian

● *to Metro Center*

● SNAPSHOT ●

The White House, official home and office of the president of the United States, and its surrounding green spaces and historical monuments evoke a strong sense of national power and history, and are vivid reminders of those who shaped America's earliest days and those who made sacrifices for the country since its turbulent beginning. Spending time at each is a real-life, hands-on way to learn American history without opening a book. During the National Cherry Blossom Festival in late March/early April, the Tidal Basin is engulfed in a cloud of pale and dark pink cherry blossoms, and the entire city celebrates. Check the map at the beginning of this chapter if you have a specific landmark in mind, and see which Metro stop brings you closest to it. However, the best way to explore DC is on foot, so don your most comfortable shoes and get going!

PLACES TO SEE
Landmarks:

TOP PICK!

The **★WHITE HOUSE (1)** *(1600 Pennsylvania Ave. NW, 202-456-2200, www.whitehouse. gov, self-guided tour hours: Tu–Th 7:30AM– 11AM, F 7:30AM–noon, Sa 7:30AM–1PM)* is probably the most recognizable building in Washington, DC, with its distinctive design by Irish-born architect James Hoban. The cornerstone was laid in 1782, and the building was finished in time for the second U.S. president, John Adams, and his wife Abigail to become the first official residents in 1800. During the War of 1812, the British torched the house, gutting the interior, but a summer thunderstorm saved the exterior from destruction. President James Madison brought Hoban back to restore the structure; after three years it was ready for occupancy. The sandstone mansion was again painted white. Theodore Roosevelt had "The White House" engraved on his official stationery in 1901, giving it the name that has endured ever since.

Few people realize how large the structure actually is. It has six stories with 132 rooms, 35 bathrooms, 28 fireplaces, a tennis court, a bowling alley, a movie theater, jogging track, and a swimming pool. In 1961, Jacqueline Kennedy, wife of the 35th president, formed

a fine arts committee to restore the landmark's well-worn furnishings to their original grandeur. Because of her efforts, the

White House (1) now enjoys a museum-like collection of antiques. A few of the public rooms are open to visitors, including the white-and-gold East Room (used for press conferences), the Green Room (used for photo shoots), and the State Dining Room, which seats 140 people.

More than 80 types of trees planted over the years by every presidential family thrive in the surrounding 18 acres. The famous Rose Garden was planted in 1913. The grounds are closed to visitors except during the Easter Egg Roll and Garden Tours.

Free White House tours are currently available for parties of 10 or more people. Tour requests must be submitted through your senator or representative *(www.senate.gov or www.house.gov)*, are accepted up to six months in advance, and are scheduled about one month in advance of your requested date. Note that you don't have to be part of a group of 10 to go on a White House tour. Your member of congress can place individuals and families with another tour group. Also, foreign visitors should check with their respective embassy for information on White House tour opportunities. Keep in mind that tours are subject to last-minute cancellation. For the most current information, call the 24-hour line: 202-456-7041.

Non-planner types do have an option. About a block away, the **White House Visitor Center (2)** *(14th St. and Constitution Ave. NW, 202-208-1631, daily 7:30AM–4PM)* offers permanent exhibits relating to the **White House (1)** and its furnishings, first families, and ceremonies. Royal gifts are also on display.

Next, head to the **Dwight D. Eisenhower Executive Office Building (3)** *(Pennsylvania Ave. and 17th St. NW, 202-395-5895, www.whitehouse.gov/about/eeob)*. Also known as the Old Executive Office Building, it was built between 1871 and 1888, and remains a major example of French Second Empire architecture. Formerly the State, War, and Navy Department Building, and once the largest office building in Washington, its granite walls exude power. You're likely to see all the president's men and women—executive branch staffers—rushing in and out.

On the grounds to the south, look skyward to see the **First Division War Memorial**. It's a tribute to the some 5,500 soldiers of the U.S. Army's First Division who lost their lives in World War I. Created by Daniel Chester French, its gilded bronze Winged Victory stands atop the striking 78-foot marble column, forming an impressive silhouette against the sky. The nearby "big red one" flower bed is planted with red tulips in spring and red begonias in summer.

 The massive Greek Revival building next to the White House on the other side is the **U.S. Treasury Building (4)** *(1500 Pennsylvania Ave. NW, 202-622-2000, www.ustreas.gov)*. This is where Andrew Johnson's temporary office was located after Lincoln's assassination. Outside is a statue of Alexander Hamilton, the department's first secretary. One hour tours are conducted Saturday mornings at 9,

9:45, 10:30, and 11:15. Advance reservations must be made through your senator or representative.

Just south of the White House and the Treasury Building is **President's Park (5)** *(the White House grounds)* and the **Ellipse (5)**, once used for sheep and cattle grazing when it was undeveloped marshland before the 1860s. At the southern end, the National Boy Scout Memorial marks the site of the first Boy Scout Jamboree in 1937. The northern edge of the park is where the living national Christmas tree, a Colorado spruce, is displayed.

As you continue walking south, you'll see the ★**WASHINGTON MONUMENT (6)** *(15th St. and Constitution Ave. NW, 202-426-6841, www. nps.gov/wamo, daily 9AM–5PM)*. The 555-foot, white marble obelisk is an imposing silhouette (it's the tallest building in DC). The monument was designed by Robert Mills and the cornerstone laid in 1848, but controversy (a commemorative stone donated by Pope Pius IX was stolen by anti-papists), lack of funds, and the Civil War halted construction on it for more than 10 years. You can see how far the initial builders got by the change of color in the stone about 150 feet up. Construction resumed in 1876 and was completed in 1884, when the monument's marble capstone was set, topped with a 9-inch aluminum tip, and wired with lightning conductors. Officially opened

to the public in 1888, the Washington Monument made a fitting memorial to founding father George Washington, first president of the United States.

The interior (made of Maine granite) features nearly 200 commemorative stones donated by U.S. states, other nations, groups, and individuals. Inserted among the granite blocks, these include stones donated by the Cherokee Nation; the New York City Fire Department; the Sultan of Turkey; the Ladies of Lowell, Massachusetts; numerous Masonic groups; and the state of Alaska, which contributed a stone of pure jade.

An iron stairway consisting of 897 steps and 50 landings leads to the observation tower, but visitors are no longer permitted to climb them. Instead, you can ride the elevator 50 stories to the top (it takes about one minute), where the 360-degree views of DC, Virginia, and Maryland are breathtaking. Fifty flags, representing each state, surround the monument's base. Individual same-day tickets are free on a first-come, first-served basis at a kiosk at the base of the monument on 15th Street NW beginning at 8AM; however, they do run out early. To purchase advance tickets, call 877-444-6777 or visit www.recreation.gov. There is a small service fee per ticket.

Several other significant monuments are clustered together between 17th and 23rd Streets NW and between Constitution and Independence Avenues NW.

In 1987, Roger Durbin of Ohio, a former Army tank mechanic under General George Patton, asked his representative, Marcy Kaptur, if a World War II memorial could be built. She introduced legislation in 1987, and again in 1989, 1991, and 1993. Finally, congress passed legislation authorizing the building of a National World War II Memorial in Washington, DC or its immediate environs; it was signed into law by president Clinton on May 25, 1993. An advisory board that included senator Bob Dole was appointed to oversee site selection and fund-raising. A design by Friedrich St. Florian of Rhode Island was selected in a competition that attracted more than 400 entries. Eleven years later, on May 29, 2004, president George W. Bush dedicated the ★NATIONAL WORLD WAR II MEMORIAL (7) *(east end of the Reflecting Pool, bet. the Lincoln Memorial and the Washington Monument, www.nps.gov/nwwm; open 24 hours, staffed daily 9:30AM–11:30PM)* in a ceremony that drew 150,000, including Tom Hanks, Tom Brokaw, and scores of WWII veterans and their families. (Sadly, Roger Durbin had passed away in 2000, but his grand-children were honored guests.)

TOP PICK!

Now one of DC's most popular sights, the 7-1/2-acre memorial, with its plaza, Freedom Wall, and Rainbow Pool, is a powerful tribute to the "Greatest Generation," the 16 million American men and women who served in the Great War, and the more than 400,000 who perished. Curved ramps provide access to the plaza for visitors walking along the east-west pathways

between the Lincoln Memorial and Washington Monument. The 17th Street ceremonial entrance is flanked by two flagpoles. Two baldachinos, or stone canopies, mark the north and south plaza entries; they feature four bronze columns with four American eagles bearing a laurel wreath, a symbol of victory. Sit along the circumference of the 246-foot Rainbow Pool and enjoy its waterworks, along with the memorial's other fountains and waterfalls; they're intended to evoke a celebratory note.

Fifty-six granite pillars, connected by a sculpted rope of bronze, symbolize each U.S. state and territory. Scenes on 24 bas-relief panels by sculptor Raymond Kaskey, and based on archival photographs, trace the war on Atlantic and Pacific fronts. From Pearl Harbor, enlistment, shipbuilding, and Rosie the Riveter, to tanks in combat, the Navy in action, the Normandy beach landings, and liberation, the story of America's transformation and unity of purpose unfolds. Visitors will also be delighted by the "Kilroy Was Here" graffiti engraved on the memorial; the cartoon figure "Kilroy" turned up on every front during WWII, confounding enemies and rallying U.S. troops.

Finally, the Freedom Wall on the western side of the memorial, with its field of 4,000 sculpted gold stars (one for approximately 100 American deaths during the war), is accompanied by the inscription, "Here we mark the price of freedom." The northwestern corner of the memorial site offers a landscaped contemplative area. The memorial is especially dramatic when illuminated at night.

Stroll by the **Reflecting Pool** *(bet. the Washington Monument and Lincoln Memorial)*, an elongated rectangle so-named because it reflects the **Washington Monument (6)** at night, and relax in **Constitution Gardens (8)** *(north of the Reflecting Pool, www.nps.gov/coga, open 24 hours)*, 45 acres of landscaped grounds, including a small lake and an island that were originally under the Potomac River. Trees and benches line the paths, creating a great place to picnic.

The haunting **★VIETNAM VETERANS MEMORIAL (9)** *(Bacon Dr. and Constitution Ave., 202-426-6841, www.nps.gov/vive, open 24 hours, staffed daily 9:30AM–11:30PM)* honors

TOP PICK!

members of the U.S. armed forces lost in America's longest, and one of its most controversial, conflicts. The black granite "V" wall lists nearly 60,000 names of those killed, missing in action, or held as prisoners of war; the names are listed in chronological order, the first dating from 1959. The memorial was conceived by the Vietnam Veterans Memorial Fund organization to make no political statement about the war; instead, its purpose is to encourage reconciliation and healing. A national competition for the memorial's design was announced in 1980; 1,421

entries were received. Number 1,026, submitted by 21-year-old Yale student Maya Ying Lin, was chosen. But Lin's stark, below-ground-level design proved as divisive as the conflict it was based on, and prolonged debate placed the fund in danger of losing its two-acre memorial site. At last, a compromise was decided—the site would include a 60-foot flagpole and two sculptures. The life-size Three Servicemen Statue, with its trio of battle-worn soldiers, represents camaraderie and reconciliation. The Vietnam Women's Memorial, a tribute to the women who served, portrays three uniformed women aiding a wounded male soldier. Eight trees around the plaza commemorate each of the military women who died in Vietnam.

A brief walk southwest will take you to the **★LINCOLN MEMORIAL (10)** *(23rd St. and Constitution Ave. NW, 202-426-6841, www.nps.gov/linc, open 24 hours, staffed daily 9:30AM–11:30PM)*, honoring the 16th president. Planning for this memorial began in 1867, two years after Lincoln's death. A symbol of American democracy and freedom, it also memorializes the conclusion of the American Civil War. Designed by Henry Bacon in 1912, and modeled after the ancient Greek Parthenon in Athens, the memorial is particularly compelling at

TOP PICK!

dawn or dusk. Its 36 Doric columns represent the states in the Union at the time of Lincoln's death. Inside the memorial is the colossal, 19-foot-high seated statue of Lincoln. Called by some "The Brooding Lincoln," this famous sculpture, designed by Daniel Chester French, weighs 175 tons. It was carved from 28 blocks of white Georgian marble. As you approach the monument, the figure seems to disappear; as you climb the stairs, Lincoln majestically comes into view. The monument's chamber is composed of limestone walls inscribed with the Gettysburg Address and Lincoln's Second Inaugural Address.

The memorial to the "Great Emancipator" is also the site of historic gatherings. In 1939, the Daughters of the American Revolution refused to allow internationally renowned African-American singer Marian Anderson to perform at their Constitution Hall (an action that prompted first lady Eleanor Roosevelt to resign from the organization). With the assistance of Mrs. Roosevelt and the "Committee for Marian Anderson," Anderson instead performed at the **Lincoln Memorial** to an audience of more than 70,000. (The D.A.R. finally invited Marian to perform for a war relief concert in 1943.)

Twenty-four years later, Martin Luther King, Jr. delivered his unforgettable "I Have a Dream" speech here after a civil rights march. Look for the words "I Have a Dream. Martin Luther King, Jr., The March on Washington for Jobs and Freedom, August 28, 1963," inscribed on the granite steps; they mark the spot where Dr. King stood.

To the southeast, you'll see the **Korean War Veterans Memorial (11)** *(West Potomac Park, Independence Ave.*

next to the Lincoln Memorial, 202-426-6841, www.nps. kwvm.com, open 24 hours, staffed daily 9:30AM– 11:30PM). Dedicated in 1995, it features 19 larger-than-life stainless steel statues of soldiers on patrol. Opposite, the 164-foot black granite wall is etched with photographic images of the war. Its polished surface reflects the statues so that there appear to be 38 of them, symbolizing the 38th parallel, the dividing line between North and South Korea. Nearby, another black wall is etched with the words, "Freedom Is Not Free."

Head farther southeast to discover the most picturesque spots in the Capital City, the **Tidal Basin (12)** *(West Basin Drive)*. Encircled by more than 3,000 cherry trees—a 1912 gift from the people of Japan—it's a local and tourist favorite. Musicians and dancers perform on the Tidal Basin stage here during the annual Cherry Blossom Festival in late March/early April. You can rent paddleboats at Tidal Basin Paddleboats *(1501 Maine Ave., SW, 202-479-2426, www.tidalbasinpaddleboat.com)*. Reserve a paddleboat in advance for an up-close view of the blossoms in early spring.

A brief walk northwest of the **Tidal Basin** will take you to the **DC World War I Memorial (13)** *(east of the Reflecting Pool, north of Independence Ave.)*, a dome over a circle of Doric columns. Dating from 1931, it commemorates local heroes of the First World War.

Located along the edge of the Tidal Basin is the National Mall's newest addition. The **Martin Luther King National Memorial (14)** *(Tidal Basin, www.mlkmemorial.org)*

dedicated in August 2011, commemorates the life and legacy of the civil rights leader.

To get to the popular **Franklin Delano Roosevelt Memorial (15)** *(1850 W. Basin Dr. SW, 202-426-6841, www.nps.gov/fdrm, open 24 hours, staffed daily 9:30AM–11:30PM)*, walk directly south toward the Potomac River. Dedicated in 1997, the FDR memorial is a tribute to the "People's President" who led the U.S. through some of its most trying times, from the Great Depression to WWII. Four outdoor galleries, arranged chronologically, depict scenes from the 32nd president's unprecedented four terms in office, featuring the New Deal, fireside chats, the attack on Pearl Harbor, and the public's shock at Roosevelt's passing at age 63, just months after his fourth inaugural.

The memorial incorporates several bronze statues, including a Depression-era breadline, first lady Eleanor Roosevelt, and Roosevelt with his beloved Scottish terrier Fala, as well as shade trees, reflecting pools, and waterfalls. Quotations by FDR are engraved into walls of red South Dakota granite. This was the first DC memorial specifically designed to be wheelchair accessible; you'll also see a statue of the president in his wheelchair at the front of the memorial, located along Cherry Tree Walk on the western edge of the Tidal Basin.

Note: You'll find a much smaller memorial to Roosevelt at 9th Street and Pennsylvania Avenue on the grounds of the National Archives. The president reportedly once said that a desk-sized block of stone placed at the Archives would suffice as his memorial. A simple marble slab was installed there in the 1960s to fulfill that original request; engraved upon it are the words, "In Memory of Franklin Delano Roosevelt 1882–1945."

Southeast of the Tidal Basin in West Potomac Park, the 2-1/2 acre ★**THOMAS JEFFERSON MEMORIAL (16)** *(Tidal Basin South End, East Basin Dr. SW, 202-426-6841, www.nps.gov/thje; open 24 hours, staffed daily 9:30AM–11:30PM)* commemorates the third U.S. President. Franklin Delano Roosevelt, who spearheaded the memorial's construction, laid the cornerstone in 1939. Designed by John Russell Pope, the open-air, marble structure emulates the classical style favored by Jefferson and resembles his own Monticello. It was dedicated on April 13, 1943, the 200th anniversary of Jefferson's birth. From the

TOP PICK!

steps, it's a stunning view of the Tidal Basin and the White House beyond.

Outside the memorial, above the entrance, you'll see a bas-relief of Jefferson with Benjamin Franklin, John Adams, Robert Livingston, and Roger Sherman, all of whom composed the Declaration of Independence. Inside, atop a six-foot pedestal of black granite, you'll find a towering, 19-foot bronze statue of Jefferson addressing the Continental Congress, a copy of the Declaration of Independence in his left hand. Sculpted by Virginia artist Rudulph Evans, who studied in France with Auguste Rodin, the statue is clad in a fur cloak given to Jefferson by friend and Revolutionary hero, the Polish general Thaddeus Kosciuszko. (Jefferson once said of Kosciuszko, "As pure a son of liberty as I have ever known.") The memorial's interior walls are inscribed with passages from Jefferson's writings, including the Declaration of Independence. A small museum beneath the monument is devoted to his legacy.

Arts & Entertainment:

The ★U.S. HOLOCAUST MEMORIAL MUSEUM (17) *(100 Raoul Wallenberg Pl. SW, 202-488-0400, www.ushmm.org, daily 10AM–5PM)* to the north is America's memorial to the millions of Jews, Poles, Jehovah's Witnesses, Gypsies, homosexuals, political prisoners, mentally and physically disabled people, and others killed by the Nazis between 1933 and 1945. The museum's permanent exhibit, "The Holocaust," is divided into three parts: Nazi Assault, Final Solution, and Last Chapter. The tour begins with eyewitness accounts by American soldiers describing what they found during the liberation of the concentration camps at the end of World War II. Each visitor is assigned an identity card of a real person from the Holocaust; throughout the tour, the card provides additional information on that person's status. The Holocaust story is told through more than 900 artifacts (including a Polish freight car like those used to transport Warsaw Jews to the Treblinka death camp), videos, historic film footage, and eyewitness accounts. A second-floor Rescuers' Wall lists the names of those who risked their lives to save Jewish men, women, and children.

The permanent exhibit is not recommended for children under 11 years of age, but those eight and older are invited to the special first-floor exhibition, "Remember the Children: Daniel's Story," an account of the Holocaust as seen through the eyes of an eight-year-old Jewish boy.

Free timed-entry passes, available on a first-come, first-served basis at opening time (in the summer lines begin forming about 8AM), are necessary to view the permanent exhibit from March–August. Passes are not needed for the permanent exhibit during the fall and winter months or for "Daniel's Story," the Wall of Remembrance, a memorial to the 1.5 million children killed during the Holocaust, or the museum's Wexner Learning Center. Advance tickets for the museum are available through the museum's website or 877-80-USHMM.

If you're traveling with children, check out the **Bureau of Engraving and Printing (18)** *(14th and C Sts. SW, 202-874-2330 or 866-874-2330, www.moneyfactory.gov; Sep–Mar tour hours: 9AM–10:45AM, 12:30PM–2PM; Apr–Aug tour hours: 9AM–10:45AM, 12:30PM–3:45PM, 5PM–7PM)*. There's a 45-minute tour every 15 minutes Monday–Friday where you can watch the printing, cutting, and stacking of the 37 million bank notes produced daily. Free, same-day timed-entry tickets are required for the tours from March–August and are issued at the ticket booth on Raoul Wallenberg Place.

Another place for kids is the **National Aquarium (19)** *(U.S. Commerce Building, 14th St. and Constitution Ave. NW, 202-482-2825, www.nationalaquarium.com, daily 9AM–5PM)*, the oldest in the country. It's located in the basement of the Commerce Building and, though small, can amuse younger children for at least an hour.

PLACES TO EAT & DRINK
Where to Eat:

A mainstay in this area for weekday breakfast and lunch is **Café du Parc (20) ($$)** *(Willard InterContinental Washington, 1401 Pennsylvania Ave. NW, 202-942-7000, www.cafedu parc.com, M–F 6:30AM–10PM, Sa–Su 7AM–10PM)*. Washington insiders as well as visitors frequent this casual French bistro for business or pleasure. At **J & G Steakhouse (21) ($$$)** *(W Hotel, 515 15th St. NW, 2020-661-2440, www.jgsteakhousewashingtondc.com, M–Th 11:45AM–2:30PM, 5PM–10PM, F 11:45AM–2:30PM, 5PM–11PM, Sa noon–2:30PM, 5PM–11PM, Su noon–2:30PM, 5PM–10PM)* renowned international chef Jean Georges Vongerichten serves signature dishes from his other restaurants in a sexy setting. **The Occidental Restaurant (22) ($$-$$$)** *(1475 Pennsylvania Ave. NW, 202-783-1475, www.occidentaldc.com, M–Sa 11:30AM–10PM)*, a historic dining venue decorated with black-and-white photos of politicos and other famous faces, serves classic American fare. News junkies take note. You too can dine at the National Press Club's restaurant, the **Fourth Estate (23) ($$-$$$)** *(529 14th St. NW, 202-662-7638, www.press.org/fourthestate, M–Sa 11:30AM–3PM, 5:30PM–8:30PM).* Just two blocks from the White House, the cuisine is New American with an emphasis

on organic and locally-sourced ingredients. **Avenue Grill (24) ($$-$$$)** at the JW Marriott *(1331 Pennsylvania Ave. NW, 202-626-6970, www.marriott.com, daily 11:30AM–10PM)* features classic American food. Opt for the rib eye steak and spinach salad. If you want a quick breakfast, lunch, or dinner, eat with the business crowd at the **Corner Bakery Café (25) ($)** *(529 14th St. NW, 202-662-7400, www.cornerbakery cafe.com, M–F 7AM–6PM, Sa–Su 8AM–4PM).* **Ebbitt Express (26) ($)** *(675 15th St. NW, 202-347-4800, www.ebbitt.com, M–F 7:30AM–5PM)* is the convenient back-door breakfast and lunch carry-out spot of the very popular Ebbitt Grill *(see next page).* If you want a quick bite, and kosher, too, try the **U.S. Holocaust Memorial Museum Café (27) ($)** *(100 Raoul Wallenberg Pl. SW, 202-488-6151, daily 8:30AM–4:30PM).* You can even pre-order a bag lunch to go if you're in a rush.

Bars & Nightlife:

Talk about a view! The **P.O.V. Roof Terrace and Lounge (28)** *(W Washington DC, 15th St.*

and Pennsylvania Ave., 202-661-2400, www.pointofview dc.com, M–Th 11AM–2AM, F 11AM–3AM, Sa noon–3AM, Su noon–2AM) offers a fabulous view of the Mall, monuments, and White House. Enjoy classic cocktails and small plates cuisine. **Old Ebbitt Grill (29)** *(675 15th St. NW, 202-347-4800, www.ebbitt.com, Su–Th 11AM–2AM, F–Sa 11AM–3AM)* is a Washington institution and its oldest bar, dating to 1856. Popular with presidents Theodore Roosevelt, Cleveland, and Grant, it's still a favorite meeting place for political insiders and celebrities. Make a reservation or be willing to wait for a table in the bar at peak hours; you won't be disappointed.

WHERE TO SHOP

This area is not a shopping mecca, but there are a handful of decent stores here. **The White House Historical Association Museum Shop (30)** located in the **White House Visitor Center (2)** *(1450 Pennsylvania Ave. NW, 202-737-8292, www.whitehousehistory.org, daily 7:30AM–4PM)* sells high quality books, art reproductions, jewelry, gifts, and toys.

Gift items, flowers, candles, pottery, and decorative arts makes **Greenworks (31)** *(1455 Pennsylvania Ave. NW, 202-393-2142, www.greenworksflorist.com, M–F 9AM–5:30PM, Sa 10AM–3PM)* great for browsing or buying. Need something special for your beloved? **Chas Schwartz & Son Jewelers (32)** *(Willard Intercontinental Washington, 1400 F St. NW, 202-737-4757, www.chas schwartzjewelers.com, M–F 10AM–6PM, Sa 10AM–5PM),*

Washington's oldest jeweler, offers diamonds, designer jewelry, and estate treasures.

WHERE TO STAY

One of the most renowned hotels in Washington is undoubtedly the Willard InterContinental Washington (33) ($$$) *(1401 Pennsylvania Ave. NW, 202-628-9100 or 800-827-1747, www.intercontinental.com)*. Designated a National Historic Landmark in 1974, it's noted for its Beaux-Arts elegance and close proximity to the White House and Capitol Hill. Take a look in its imposing hallway lobby, stretching from the 14th and F Street entrance to the main entrance on Pennsylvania Avenue.  Lobbyists have packed this spot since the mid 1800s to hash out issues of the day. Just a block away is the W Washington D.C. (34) ($$$) *(15th St. and Pennsylvania Ave., 202-661-2400, www.starwoodhotels.com)*, offering a boutique hotel experience that combines modern style with the art of hospitality. But you don't have to be a hotel guest to enjoy the pampering services at the **Bliss Spa**. Closer to the Metro center, JW Marriott (35) ($$$) *(1331 Pennsylvania Ave. NW, 202-393-2000 or 800-228-9290, www.jwmarriottdc.com)* is convenient to the White House and the adjacent business district. The views and location are so good that the bright, spacious rooms are almost an afterthought.

● ● *to McPherson Square*

● SNAPSHOT ●

If you want to learn about the history and culture of the capital city, you can't miss if you spend some time in Lafayette Square and its surroundings. Gaze at the White House looming in front of you, and imagine past presidents politicking in these very same places. The wide-open, seven-acre green space located between H Street and Pennsylvania Avenue and between 15th and 17th Streets NW was once owned by Edward Pearce; his farmhouse was near the northeast corner of the square. An apple orchard and a family burial ground were located here in the late 1600s, but the federal government took title of the land in 1792 when construction of the capital city was underway. Statues of four men from foreign countries who served as generals in the Revolutionary War mark each of the square's corners: the Marquis de Lafayette, the Comte de Rochambeau, Baron von Steuben, and Thaddeus Kosciuszko. In contemporary times, the square is the site of celebrations and protests.

PLACES TO SEE

Landmarks:

Begin your exploration just north of Lafayette Square at **St. John's Episcopal Church (36)** *(16th and H Sts. NW, www.stjohns-dc.org)*, built in 1816 by architect Benjamin Latrobe. With its bright yellow stuccoed walls and golden yellow cupola and dome, it is difficult to miss. Every president since James Madison has worshipped here at some point, traditionally in pew 54. As you walk south, don't miss the striking views of the White House before you. In the center of Lafayette Square stands Clark Mills's **Equestrian Statue of President Andrew Jackson (37)**, erected in 1853. Stop at the southeast corner of the park to view the **Statue of Lafayette (38)**, turning right and continuing in front of the White House until you reach the **Blair House (39)** *(1651–1653 Pennsylvania Ave. NW)*. Owner Francis Preston Blair (1791–1876) was the founder and editor of the *Washington Globe* from 1830–1845. In the 1940s, the house became the official residence of visiting dignitaries and, during White House remodeling, President Harry S. Truman moved here temporarily. Walk north along the square on Jackson Place to the **Decatur House (40)** *(748 Jackson Pl. NW)*, one of the oldest houses in DC. Congressmen, businessmen, politicians, and diplomats chose the address as a residence for its proximity to the White House. As you walk south, you'll see the **Octagon House (41)** *(1799 New York Ave. NW)*, built for plantation owner John Taylor III in 1801. President

Madison and his wife lived here when the White House was burned in the War of 1812. During the Civil War, General George McClellan used it as his headquarters, and in 1897, during

the William McKinley administration, Vice President Garret Augustus Hobart leased it, hence the name, "Little White House." Now the building is owned by the American Architectural Foundation.

Arts & Entertainment:

When you tire of politics, history, and government, choose among the many museums near Lafayette Square, all within 10–15 minutes of each other. Start at the **Renwick Gallery of the Smithsonian American Art Museum (42)** *(Pennsylvania Ave. at 17th St. NW, 202-633-1000, www.americanart.si.edu, 10AM–5:30PM)* for

a trip into the world of American crafts and decorative arts from the 19th–21st centuries. The Grand Salon on the second floor is the re-creation of a 19th-century collector's gallery. And look for cool con-

temporary works, like *Game Fish*, a collage fashioned from toys and game pieces. Next, walk south on 17th Street for a few minutes and find the **Corcoran Gallery of Art (43)** *(500 17th St. NW, entrance on 17th, New York/E St., 202-639-1700, www.corcoran.org, W, F–Su 10AM–5PM, Th 10AM–9PM)*, which houses an extensive collection of American masterworks and European and contemporary art. The Corcoran moved to this space, a French Beaux-Arts structure with

Greek-inspired details, in 1897. Designed by Ernest Flagg, who is also responsible for the U.S. Naval Academy at Annapolis, it houses the **Corcoran College of Art + Design**, which adjoins the gallery.

You can visit the **American Red Cross Visitors Center (44)** *(430 17th St., 202-303-7066, www.redcross.org/museum; guided tour hours: W and F 10AM and 2PM, Sa noon and 2PM)* to explore the role of the Red Cross in disaster relief and emergency preparedness. The **Daughters of the American Revolution Museum (45)** *(1776 D St. NW, 202-879-3241, www.dar.org/museum, M–F 9:30AM–4PM, Sa 9AM–5PM)*, one block south, includes more than 30 period-decorated rooms, among them a one-room Pilgrim dwelling, a Victorian parlor, a tavern, and an attic filled with toys and dolls. Next door, **DAR Constitution Hall (46)** *(311 18th St. NW; open to the public during performances)*, a venue for concerts and other performing arts, is the largest auditorium in DC. To view Latin American and Caribbean art, stop at the **Art Museum of the Americas (47)** *(201 18th St. NW, 202-458-6016, www.museum.oas.org, Tu–Su 10AM–5PM)*, part of the Organization of American States. The Spanish colonial-style building dates from 1912. Behind the house, the seasonal plant display and blue-tiled pool comprise a not so hidden "secret" DC garden.

PLACES TO EAT & DRINK
Where to Eat:

Pining for pastrami on rye? **Loeb's Deli Restaurant (48) ($)** *(1712 I St. NW, 202-965-5632, M–F 6:30AM–4:30PM, no dinner service)* will make you feel at

home right away. **Pedro and Vinny's (49) ($)** *(1500 K. St. NW, 571-237-1875, www.pedroandvinnys.com, weekday lunch hours only)*, a food cart, offers super-fresh vegetarian burritos. Order yours with habanero sauce, and head over to one of the benches at Lafayette Square to enjoy in the shadow of the White House. **Ici (50) ($$$)** *(Sofitel Lafayette Square, 806 15th St. NW, 202-730-8700, www.icibistro.com, M–F 6:30AM–10PM, Sa–Su 7AM– 11AM, 6PM–10PM)* is a *très bon* bistro serving stylish country French cuisine in a relaxed setting. With long hours and a wide-ranging menu from breakfast to late night, it's a delightful stop in this part of town. Rub shoulders with politicians, journalists, lawyers, lobbyists, and former presidents at **The Oval Room (51) ($$)** *(800 Connecticut Ave., 202-463-8700, www.ovalroom.com,*

M–F 11:30AM–3PM, dinner M–Th 5:30PM–10PM, F–Sa 5:30PM–10:30PM). The dining room is a dramatic, modern space and the cuisine is American with a Mediterranean twist. Try

Georgia Brown's (52) ($$-$$$) *(950 15th St. NW, 202-393-4499, www.gbrowns.com, M–Th 11:30AM–10PM, F 11:30AM–11PM, Sa noon–11PM, Su brunch 10AM–2:30PM,* *dinner 5:30PM–11PM)* for southern cuisine inspired by the South Carolina low country. Catfish fingers, Carolina gumbo, or shrimp and grits are some of their specialties. Live jazz on Saturday evenings and Sunday brunch. Stop at **Caribou Coffee (53) ($)** *(17th and Pennsylvania Ave., www.cariboucoffee.com, 202-466-2905, M–F 6AM–7PM, Sa 8AM–7PM, Su 8AM–5PM)* directly across from the White House to relax and unwind the way the wonks do—over a newspaper or brief. For a drink

other than coffee, among your best winter choices is the Apple Blast—hot cider, whipped cream, caramel, and cinnamon blended into a frothy liquid. In summer, choose a cooler—caramel, chocolate, or vanilla. For Spanish cuisine amid tapestries and lace, reserve a table at **Taberna del Alabardero (54) ($$$)** *(1776 I St. at 18th St. NW, 202-429-2200, www.alabardero.com, M–F 11:30AM–2:30PM, 5:30PM–10:30PM, Sa 5:30PM–10:30PM)*. Deemed by the Spanish government to be the "Best Spanish Restaurant Outside of Spain," this gem offers lobster, seafood paella, and tapas—the real thing! For a fun meal, head to

Potbelly Sandwich Works (55) ($) *(1400 New York Ave. at 14th St. NW, 202-628-9500, www.potbelly.com, M–F 11AM–7PM, Sa–Su 11AM–4PM)*. It seems everyone who works in the neighborhood comes here; it also serves shakes, malts, yogurt smoothies, chili, and soups.

Café Asia (56) ($-$$) *(1720 I St. NW, 202-659-2696, www.cafe asia.com, M–Th 11:30AM–10PM, F–Sa 11:30AM–midnight, Su 11:30AM–10PM)* has a big fol-

lowing for its Japanese, Thai, and Chinese cuisine. Sushi fans find uncomplicated maki and sashimi with fresh flavors and low prices.

For **Bars & Nightlife**, try the neighboring **Downtown** area (see page 129).

WHERE TO SHOP

The gift shops at many of the museums are worth a trip for their unusual, high-quality items. The **Decatur House (40)** *(748 Jackson Pl. NW, 202-842-0920, M–Sa 10AM–5PM, Su noon–4PM)* has a diverse array of histori-cally relevant items, such as Salisbury pewter and the White House china collection. The **Renwick Gallery (42)** *(Pennsylvania Ave. at 17th St. NW, 202-633-1000, daily 10AM–5:30PM)* sells jewelry, handmade crafts, and books. The **Corcoran Gallery of Art (43)** *(500 17th St. NW, 202-639-1700, W, F–Su 10AM–5PM, Th 10AM–9PM, closed M–Tu)* has unique toys, jewelry, and apparel. Even more merchandise inspired by his-tory can be found at **Daughters of the American Revolution Museum (45)** *(1776 D St. NW, 202-879-3241, M–F 9:30AM–4PM, Sa 9AM–5PM)*, which sells jewelry, clothing, and toys and crafts.

WHERE TO STAY

The posh hotels here are considered pricey, but you'll love the VIP treatment. Stay at the **Hay-Adams Hotel (57) ($$$)** *(16th and H St. NW, 202-638-6600, or 800-853-6807, www.hayadams.com)* for the quintessential Washington experience—understated and elegant. The Hay-Adams was the Obama family's temporary home in the weeks leading up to the 2009 inauguration. Named for John Milton Hay and Henry Brooks Adams, past owners of the adjoining houses on the site, the hotel is reminiscent of the 1920s but somehow stays current. Ask the lobby staff to see the roof terrace used for receptions and weddings—it affords a grand White House view.

The **St. Regis Washington, DC (58) ($$$)** *(923 16th St. and K St. NW, 202-638-2626, or 866-716-8116, www.stregis.com/washington)* pampers its guests with everything they could ever want. Dine at **Adour**, Alain Ducasse's DC location. The spacious, Old World-style lobby is ideal for a confidential conversation.

For a more contemporary environment and a different kind of experience, stay at the **Sofitel Lafayette Square (59) ($$-$$$)** *(806 15th St. NW, 202-730-8800, www.sofitel.com)*, DC's only 4-diamond French hotel, housed in a historic building dating from 1880. It boasts over 200 rooms and 16 suites, with exceptionally large windows. The sleek lobby is an airy place, perfect for early morning meetings.

All around . . . the meticulous geometry of streets and monuments radiated outward. Even from the air, Washington, D.C., exuded an almost mystical power.

—*Dan Brown*, The Lost Symbol

chapter 2

NATIONAL MALL

CAPITOL HILL

Places to See:

1. The Castle
2. Enid A. Haupt Garden
3. NATIONAL MUSEUM OF AMERICAN HISTORY ★
4. National Museum of Natural History
5. National Gallery of Art Sculpture Garden
6. NATIONAL GALLERY OF ART, WEST BUILDING ★
7. NATIONAL GALLERY OF ART, EAST BUILDING ★
8. National Museum of the American Indian
9. Voice of America
10. Washington Design Center
11. NATIONAL AIR AND SPACE MUSEUM ★
12. Joseph Hirshhorn Museum and Sculpture Garden
13. National Museum of African Art
14. Arthur M. Sackler Gallery
15. Freer Gallery of Art
24. U.S. CAPITOL BUILDING ★
25. U.S. Botanic Garden
26. Capitol Reflecting Pool
27. Ulysses S. Grant Memorial
28. SUPREME COURT OF THE UNITED STATES ★
29. LIBRARY OF CONGRESS ★
30. Folger Shakespeare Library
31. Sewall-Belmont House and Museum
32. Union Station
33. National Postal Museum
34. Barracks Row

Places to Eat & Drink:

16. Wright Place Food Court
17. Mitsitam Café
18. Cascade Café Espresso & Gelato Bar
19. Garden Café
20. Atrium Café
21. Stars and Stripes Café
22. Jazz in the Garden
35. The Monocle
36. Charlie Palmer Steak
37. Taqueria Nacional
38. B. Smith's
39. America
40. Market Lunch
41. Bistro Bis

★ *Top Pick*

42. Sonoma
43. Montmartre
44. White Tiger
45. Café Berlin
46. The Dubliner
47. Hawk & Dove
48. Banana Café & Piano Bar

Where to Shop:

Smithsonian Retail Stores
(located in individual museums)
49. Eastern Market
50. Groovy DC
51. East Hall

Where to Stay:

23. Holiday Inn Capitol
52. Hotel George
53. Hyatt Regency Washington
on Capitol Hill
54. Phoenix Park Hotel
55. Capitol Hill Suites
56. Liaison Capitol Hill
57. Washington Court Hotel on
Capitol Hill

All is politics in this capital.

—Thomas Jefferson

⬤ ⬤ *to Smithsonian, or Federal Triangle*

⬤ ⬤ ⬤ ⬤ *to L'Enfant Plaza*

• SNAPSHOT •

The Mall is a treasure trove of riches in sciences, the arts, history, and cultures from around the world. It's not a mall as in shopping, but a grassy area extending from the Capitol to the Washington Monument, surrounded by a collection of world-class museums that can transport you to the past, the future, to foreign nations, and back again to the United States. Whatever your passion, you will find it here. Because there is so much to do and see, familiarize yourself with the overall content of the Mall, then determine your priorities so you won't be overwhelmed on your first visit. Decide if you want your experience to be broad or deep. If you have lots of time, maybe it can be both, but most people have to choose.

The Mall hosts a myriad of seasonal attractions and events. For example, in winter, the central fountain of the National Gallery of Art Sculpture Garden turns into an ice rink. In summer, the Folklife Festival moves into full swing. And, when weather permits, the carousel next to the Smithsonian

Castle is a delight for the young, and not so young. If you want diversity, spend a few hours or a few days at the Mall. You'll go home a different person.

PLACES TO SEE
Landmarks:
The Castle (1), also known as the Smithsonian Institution Building *(10th St. and Independence Ave. SW, 202-633-1000, www.si.edu/museums/smithsonian-institution-building or www.si.edu, daily 8:30AM–5:30PM)*, was designed by James Renwick, Jr. The red sandstone landmark was the Smithsonian's first building, completed in 1855. It houses the Institution's Information Center and provides a 10-minute film overview of the Smithsonian. Facing the Castle is the **Enid A. Haupt Garden (2)** *(10th St. and Independence Ave. SW)*, 4-plus acres of formal gardens sprinkled with 1870s cast-iron furnishings. Most visitors are unaware that this is a rooftop garden (on ground level) that spans the roofs of the subterranean National Gallery of African Art and the Sackler Gallery.

Arts & Entertainment:
The museums of the Smithsonian Institution dominate the National Mall. James Smithson (1765–1829), an English scientist who had never been to the United States, left more than $500,000 to the fledgling country to found the Smithsonian. In his lifetime, he had conducted research in chemistry, mineralogy, and geology. Since 1829, his legacy has spawned many new museums.

How and from where you approach the Mall depends on your interests. There is something for everyone, and almost all of the museums have exhibits that appeal to children. Best of all admission is free. Note too that during the spring and summer, many of the museums have extended evening hours. If you begin your Mall explorations at the west end, nearest the Washington Monument, the first building you'll find is the ★NATIONAL MUSEUM OF AMERICAN HISTORY (3) *(14th St. and Constitution Ave. NW, 202-633-1000, americanhistory.si.edu, daily 10AM–5:30PM)* which boasts a light-filled atrium, a grand glass staircase, and a state-of-the-art gallery to display the museum's prized possession—the flag that inspired the United States' national anthem, "The Star-Spangled Banner." Also on display is the White House copy of President Lincoln's Gettysburg Address. **America on the Move** uses sights and sounds to re-create the history of transportation in the United States from 1870 to the present.

Four levels of exhibitions can leave you exhausted, so stop by the second floor information desk when you arrive to see what's new, what interests you, and where it is located. If you're traveling with children, check out the **Spark! Lab**, where kids can conduct experiments. The museum's collection of popular entertainment artifacts is a highlight that captivates across generations. View the ruby slippers worn by Judy Garland in *The Wizard of Oz*, Jim Henson's Kermit the Frog puppet,

TOP PICK!

and Seinfeld's "puffy shirt." See the controversial 1840 sculpture of George Washington wearing a toga. The Gowns of the First Ladies is another popular exhibit.

Next door, the mammoth **National Museum of Natural History (4)** *(Constitution Ave. at 10th St. NW, 202-633-1000, www.mnh.si.edu, daily 10AM–5:30PM)*, houses beaucoup wonders of the natural world under its dome. Henry, an African elephant, sits at the museum's crossroads in the first-floor rotunda; he makes an ideal meeting spot. The Hall of Mammals is extraordinary. Check out the highly interactive Sant Ocean Hall. Or take in an IMAX movie, ooh and ah over the 23.1-carat Carmen Lúcia ruby, or take the kids to see the Tyrannosaurus rex face off with a Triceratops.

If it's time for a break, stop next door at the **National Gallery of Art Sculpture Garden (5)** *(9th St. and Constitution Ave. NW, www.nga.gov, M–Sa 10AM–5PM, Su 11AM–6PM)* and relax at the fountain and reflecting pool. Mid-November through mid-March, the garden is transformed into an outdoor ice-skating rink. Adjacent to the garden is the ★**NATIONAL GALLERY OF ART, WEST BUILDING (6)** *(6th St. and Constitution Ave. NW, 202-737-4215, www.nga.gov, M–Sa 10AM–5PM, Su 11AM–6PM)*, home to major special exhibitions and a permanent collection of European and American

TOP PICK!

paintings, sculpture, decorative arts, and works on paper. This domed neoclassical building was designed by John Russell Pope in 1941. There are more than 100 galleries in this foremost collection. It is the only museum in the United States to display a painting by Leonardo da Vinci, a portrait of *Ginevra de' Benci* in Gallery 6. Some other highlights are Rembrandt's *The Mill* in Gallery 48, Monet's *Rouen Cathedral* in the west façade, and *Sunlight* in Gallery 85. For a more contemporary experience, head to the ★**NATIONAL GALLERY OF ART, EAST BUILDING (7)** *(4th St. and Constitution Ave. NW, 202-737-4215, www.nga.gov, M–Sa 10AM–5PM, Su 11AM–6PM)*, designed by architect I. M. Pei (who designed the famous Paris Louvre pyramid), and home of the renowned 76-foot-long Alexander Calder mobile (*Untitled*, 1976) suspended from the ceiling of the atrium. It was one of his last commissions. View the permanent modern art collections and keep your eyes open for any special exhibitions of international import. There are works from most of the famous artists from the 20th century on display here, including Roy Lichtenstein, Georgia O'Keeffe, Pablo Picasso, and Jackson Pollock. Don't miss the gallery of Henri Matisse's large, colorful paper cutouts.

TOP PICK!

As you cross the Mall you'll see the newest addition to this area—the **National Museum of the American Indian (8)** *(4th St. and Independence Ave. SW, 202-633-1000, www.americanindian.si.edu, daily*

10AM–5:30PM). At the entrance you'll see and hear the word "welcome" in hundreds of Native American languages. If there's time, take in the short introductory film, *Who We Are*, in the Lelawi Theater on the 4th floor. The museum showcases beadwork, pottery, textiles, paintings, and sculptures, and is the largest in the world devoted to American Indian art and objects. The U.S. government's international broadcasting service, **Voice of America (9)** *(330 Independence Ave. SW, tour reservations 202-203-4990, www.voatours.com, tours M–F at noon and 3PM)*, broadcasts radio, television, and Internet programs in more than 45 languages to much of the world; its offices are near the Federal Center SW Metro stop. Families with children can request a kid's version of the tour, recommended for children ages 7 and up. Browse high-end home design and home furnishing showrooms open to the public at the **Washington Design Center (10)** *(300 D St. SW, 202-646-6100, www.dcdesigncenter.com, M–F 9AM–5PM)*, closest to the Federal SW Metro stop on the Orange and Blue Lines. Check out more than 70 design showrooms to see domestic and international home furnishings, fabrics, and accessories.

TOP PICK!

Continuing clockwise back toward the Mall, you'll see the ★**NATIONAL AIR AND SPACE MUSEUM (11)** *(6th St. and Independence Ave. SW, 202-633-1000, www.nasm.si.edu, daily 10AM–5:30PM)*. The most-visited museum in the world, it immerses children and adults in the

history of aviation and the space program. The first-floor exhibit, "Space Race," details the race to the moon between the Americans and the Soviets beginning in the early 1960s.
View a variety of space suits, including one worn by U.S. astronaut John Glenn on his 1962 orbital flight. "Milestones of Flight" chronicles aviation firsts, including the flight of Charles Lindbergh across the Atlantic in 1927. Spend time wandering. See the Wright Brothers' 1903 flyer and the Apollo 11 command module *Columbia*. Touch a lunar rock. Walk through a Skylab space station. Take the kids to the

Lockheed Martin IMAX Theater to see *To Fly!*, the museum's thrilling and most popular film. You'll enjoy it, too. For an IMAX movie schedule, call 202-633-IMAX (4629). To view even more jets and rockets, visit the Air and Space Museum's companion exhibit hall, the **Steven F. Udvar-Hazy Center** *(14390 Air and Space Museum Parkway, Chantilly, Virginia, 202-633-2370, www.nasm.si.edu/museum/udvarhazy, daily 10AM– 5:30PM)* near Washington Dulles International Airport. This mammoth facility showcases 127 aircraft and 143 large space artifacts—old, new, and experimental—including the Lockheed SR-71 Blackbird, the fastest jet in the world; the Boeing B-29 Superfortress *Enola Gay* bomber (used in the atomic mission that destroyed Hiroshima); and the first Space Shuttle, the *Enterprise*. You can also attend IMAX films here and watch air traffic at Dulles Airport from the Center's 164-foot Observation Tower.

For a complete change of atmosphere, next door to the air and space museum you'll find the **Joseph Hirshhorn Museum and Sculpture Garden (12)** *(7th St. and Independence Ave. SW, 202-633-1000, www.hirshhorn. si.edu, daily 10AM–5:30PM, Sculpture Garden 7:30AM– dusk)*. The cylindrical venue is devoted to 19th- and 20th-century paintings and sculpture and has an adjoining outdoor sunken garden. Don't miss Rodin's *The Burghers of Calais*. If you're traveling with kids, pick up a family guide packet with cards describing the different works in the permanent collection.

As you continue west, you'll come upon two smaller, specialized museums. *The* **National Museum of African Art (13)** *(950 Independence Ave. SW, 202-633-4600, http://africa.si.edu, daily 10AM–5:30PM)* greets visitors with the sounds of traditional and contemporary African music. The only American museum devoted to African art, it covers more than 900 cultures from the African continent and includes sculpture, textiles, household objects, decorative arts, and musical instruments. On the west side is the **Arthur M. Sackler Gallery (14)** *(1050 Independence Ave. SW, 202-633-4880, www.asia.si.edu, daily 10AM–5:30PM)*, where you can enjoy Islamic metalwork, Japanese screens, and more. Look for *Grasping for the Moon*, an intriguing work by Chinese-born expatriate Xu Bing. The "Luxury Arts of the Silk Route Empires" exhibit is located in underground galleries connecting the **Sackler Gallery (14)** to the **Freer Gallery of Art (15)** *(Jefferson Dr. at 12th St. SW, 202-633-4880, www.asia.si.edu, daily 10AM–5:30PM)*. Visit the iridescent **Peacock Room** created by James McNeill Whistler for wealthy ship owner Frederick R. Leyland in 1876. The gold- and silver-painted south wall mural depicts two fighting peacocks. The birds' brightly colored stone eyes always fascinate young children.

PLACES TO EAT & DRINK
Where to Eat:

For food and drink while you're exploring the Mall, head for cafés within the Smithsonian Museums and the National Gallery. They're convenient and quick. Try the **Wright Place Food Court (16) ($)** *(National Air and Space Museum, 6th St. at Independence Ave. SW, 202-633-1000, daily 10AM–5PM)* for kid-friendly selections from McDonald's, Donatos Pizza, and Boston Market. You will also find a café offering sandwiches, salads, and soups, plus an outdoor kiosk, weather permitting. **Mitsitam Café (17) ($)** *(National Museum of the American Indian, 4th St. and Independence Ave. SW, 202-633-1000, www.americanindian.si.edu, daily 10AM–5PM)* means "Let's Eat!" in the language of the Delaware and Piscataway people—and is perhaps the best museum café on the mall, serving regional Native American food. Do a walk-through first—there are many good choices, including sea bass ceviche, cedar plank salmon, and buffalo chili, as well as desserts, snacks, and beverages. For more fuel to keep your museum momentum going, stop at **Cascade Café Espresso & Gelato Bar (18) ($)** *(National Gallery of Art, East Building, 4th St. and Constitution Ave. NW, 202-737-4215, www.nga.gov; café: M–Sa 11AM–3PM, Su 11AM–4PM, espresso & gelato: M–Sa 10AM–4:30PM, Su 11AM–5:30PM).* The café and espresso bar are next to each other on the lower, concourse level

of the East Building. Either spot is a good place to relax and decide what to do next as you sample salads, soups, and wood-fired pizza. If you'd like more of a meal, head over to the **Garden Café (19) ($)** *(National Gallery of Art, West Building, 6th St. and Constitution Ave. NW, 202-737-4215, www.nga.gov, M–Sa 11:30AM–3PM, Su noon–4PM).* The **Atrium Café (20) ($)** *(National Museum of Natural History, Constitution Ave. at 10th St. NW, 202-633-1000, www.mnh.si.edu, M–F 11AM–3PM, Sa 11AM–5PM, Su 11AM–4PM)* focuses on eco-friendly edibles at fast-food prices—pizzas topped with local ingredients, fresh salads, and organic fruit. Lunch standbys, such as hamburgers and hot dogs, are available, too. The

Stars and Stripes Café (21) ($) *(National Museum of American History, 14th St. and Constitution Ave. NW, 202-633-1000, www.americanhistory.si.edu, daily 11AM–3PM)* offers barbecue, pizza, burgers, and

more; **Constitution Café** *(daily 10AM–5:30PM)*, also in the National Museum of American History on the first floor, features coffee, light lunches, and ice cream.

Bars & Nightlife:

There is nightlife at the Smithsonian Museums. The Smithsonian Resident Associate Program (*www.residentassociates.org*) sponsors lectures and cultural performances at several of the Smithsonian Museums throughout the year that often include receptions with food and/or drinks.

On Friday evenings throughout the summer, check out the very popular (and free!) **Jazz in the Garden (22)** series. *(National Gallery of Art Sculpture Garden, 9th St. and Constitution Ave. NW, www.nga.gov/programs/jazz, 5PM–8:30PM).* Listen and dance to jazz under the stars, performed by well-known local and regional artists. Refreshments are available for purchase, too.

For more **Bars & Nightlife**, check out the **Capitol Hill** area (see page 82).

WHERE TO SHOP

Every Smithsonian museum has at least one shop, known collectively as the Smithsonian Retail Stores, where you can shop for posters, jewelry, toys, crafts, books, and other international gift items. You can feel good knowing that your purchase supports the Smithsonian Institution's mission—"the increase and diffusion of knowledge." The museum shops are great places to find something unique and of high quality, and all are tax-free.

WHERE TO STAY

There are many hotels that are not too far from the Mall, but only one just off it: **Holiday Inn Capitol (23) ($$)** *(550 C St. SW, 202-479-4000, www.holidayinncapitol.com)* has renovated, well-appointed rooms, an outdoor seasonal rooftop pool, and a convenient location just a short walk from the Air and Space Museum as well as the Metro, making this hotel an ideal choice for families.

●● *to Capitol South, or Eastern Market*

● *to Union Station*

● SNAPSHOT ●

Capitol Hill is a diverse, fascinating part of the city, where the government's legislative and judicial branches do their work. It is home to the U.S. Capitol, the U.S. Supreme Court, Library of Congress, and the House and Senate office buildings. But it is more than that. It is one of the liveliest and oldest neighborhoods in the city as well. And, with Union Station on its northern border, it is a key gateway to and from the city—intercity and high-speed trains arrive and depart every few minutes. To really enjoy this area, try not to get stuck in the government buildings unless you are a political aficionado. Consider taking the free 45-minute tour of the Capitol, but save some time to see how the rest of the world lives in the Capitol Hill Historic District. Walk the streets and take in the architectural styles. Visit the National Postal Museum. Browse Eastern Market, the city's oldest public market, dating from 1873.

PLACES TO SEE
Landmarks:

Welcome to one of the most historic and most important structures in the United States! The

★ **U.S. CAPITOL BUILDING (24)** *(Capitol Hill, east end of the National Mall, 202-225-6827, www.visitthecapitol.gov, M–Sa 8:30AM–4:30PM)* is the focal point of the greater Capitol Complex, including six Congressional office buildings and three Library of Congress buildings. The history of the Capitol building reflects the history of America. From the time of George Washington, it's been raised up, burnt down, reconstructed, and remodeled to adapt to a nation on the move. Today, this neoclassical structure's floor area covers more than 16 acres. Start your visit with a stroll of the building's inviting 68-acre campus; it's green and parklike, yet offers unobstructed views of the Capitol itself. This was the intent of its landscape architect, the famous Frederick Law Olmsted, who felt the grounds should be "subsidiary to the central structure." Many of the trees—especially in the eastern part of the grounds—are historic, having been planted by notable individuals and groups, or donated by various states.

A West Indies physician and amateur architect, William Thornton, won the competition to design the Capitol edifice, which resembles the Pantheon in Rome. George Washington laid the cornerstone in a Masonic ceremony in 1793; the stone has since gone missing. The initial construction of the Capitol was completed in 1800, and congress held its first session there on November 17. In 1814, much of the interior was destroyed during the British "Burning of Washington." The Capitol was reconstructed the next year, and, several decades later, north and south wings were added. In 1866, a new fireproof cast-iron dome replaced the earlier dome made of copper-covered wood. This newer, distinctive dome is crowned by a 15,000-pound, 19-1/2-foot bronze Statue of Freedom, a classical female figure that represents the victory of freedom in peace and war. It is said she faces east so that symbolically, "the sun never sets on freedom." The figure holds a U.S. shield and laurel victory wreath, wears a sword, and is capped with a helmet encircled by stars and topped with an eagle's head, feathers, and talons. The sculpture was set in place in December 1863 to a 35-gun salute that was answered by the guns of 12 forts around DC. If congress is in session, you'll notice a light below the statue. (Flags also fly over the Capitol's south house side and/or senate north side in session.)

Inside the Capitol, the circular Rotunda, used for special state occasions, is lined with paintings and friezes of scenes from America's history; its "eye" features a mammoth fresco, *The Apotheosis of Washington*, depicting Washington rising to heaven. Painted in 1865 by Italian artist Constantino Brumidi, the work covers more than 4,600 square feet, and incorporates figures up to 15 feet tall. The crypt space below the rotunda is used as an exhibition space. In the National Statuary Hall (the Old

Hall of the House), you'll find statues of celebrated Americans—from Samuel Adams to Brigham Young—contributed by each of the 50 states.

Located under the East Capitol grounds, the brand-new subterranean **Capitol Visitor Center**, the "CVC," is now the Capitol's new main entrance. This expansive facility houses a theater that shows the 13-minute orientation film, *Out of Many, One*. It also broadcasts live feeds when congress is in session, boasts an exhibition gallery highlighting the Capitol's history, a 600-seat cafeteria, and gift shops. To take the Capitol Building tour, you have several options. Tours can be booked online *(www.visitthecapitol.gov)*. Some representative and senate offices offer staff-led constituent tours. Finally, there is also a limited number of same-day, timed-entry passes available at the kiosks at the east and west front entrances of the Capitol and also at the information desk at the lower level of the CVC.

Afterward, visit the **U.S. Botanic Garden (25)** *(1st St. and Independence Ave. SW, 202-225-8333, www.usbg.gov, daily 10AM–5PM)*, which features a stunning two-story glass conservatory that houses a prodigious collection of

orchids as well as the aptly named "jungle," an area filled with seasonal tropical and subtropical plants and trees; it includes a 24-foot-high viewing walkway. The **National Garden** next door features unusual plants that grow well in the mid-Atlantic region. It also contains a butterfly garden and a rose garden. Between the garden and the Capitol you'll find the **Capitol Reflecting Pool (26)** *(directly west of the Capitol)* and the **Ulysses S. Grant Memorial (27)** *(adjacent to the Capitol Reflecting Pool)*. Sculpted by Henry Shrady, it is one of the world's most intricate equestrian statues and represents the Civil War Union victory engineered by General Grant.

East of, and within easy walking distance from the capitol building, you'll find the **★SUPREME COURT OF THE UNITED STATES (28)** *(1st and E. Capitol Sts. NE, 202-479-3030, www.supremecourtus.gov, M–F 9AM–4:30PM)*. You may be surprised to learn that the court's familiar "Temple of Justice" building, its main steps flanked by the sculpted figures *Contemplation of Justice* and *Guardian of Law*, dates back only to 1935. Even though the supreme court was established in 1789, it had no official home, and met initially in the nation's first capital, New York City, then in Philadelphia, then in the DC Capitol. Finally, in 1929, former president and then Chief Justice William Howard Taft persuaded congress to authorize construction of a permanent home for the Court. Popular American architect Cass Gilbert was asked to design "a building of dignity and importance." Gilbert chose a classical Corinthian style that would complement nearby congressional buildings. But Taft and Gilbert died before the building was finished, and construction was

TOP PICK!

completed under chief justice Charles Evans Hughes, Cass Gilbert, Jr., and John R. Rockart.

At the court's impressive west side entrance, which faces the Capitol, you'll see a pair of marble candelabra flanking the steps leading to the oval plaza in front. Carved panels on the candelabra bases depict *Justice* with sword and scales, and *The Three Fates* weaving the thread of life. Sixteen marble columns support the pediment; the words "Equal Justice Under Law" appear on the architrave above. A sculptured group over the architrave features *Liberty Enthroned*; she is guarded by *Order and Authority*. Three figures on either side of this trio, sculpted by Robert Aitken, depict the concepts of council and research. To the left, you'll see chief justice Taft as a

youth, secretary of state Elihu Root, and architect Cass Gilbert. On the right are chief justice Hughes, Aitken himself, and chief justice Marshall as a young man. (Few visitors see the pediment sculpture groups on the building's east side, by Hermon MacNeil. They depict the great lawgivers Moses, Confucius, and the Greek Solon, surrounded by figures representing means of enforcing the law, tempering justice with mercy, and other court concerns. Here, the architrave says, "Justice the Guardian of Liberty.")

The court's bronze entrance doors weigh 6-1/2 tons each. Their panels depict historic scenes in the development of law: the shield of Achilles trial scene from the *Iliad*; a

Roman praetor publishing an edict; King John sealing the Magna Carta; Lord Coke barring King James from sitting as a judge; and chief justice Marshall and justice Joseph Story. Inside, double rows of marble columns line the Great Hall, and busts of former chief justices are set in niches and on marble pedestals along the wall. At the east end of the great hall, oak doors open into the court chamber itself, an 82- by 91-foot room with a 44-foot ceiling, 24 columns of Siena marble, mahogany furnishings, and Beaux-Arts friezes of 18 historic lawgivers, from Egyptian king Menes, Moses, and Draco to Charlemagne, John Marshall, and Napoleon.

The public can see the court in session. Beginning the first Monday in October, the court hears two one-hour arguments a day, on Mondays, Tuesdays, and Wednesdays in two-week intervals through late April. Argument calendars are posted on the court Web site *(www.supreme courtus.gov)* under the "Oral Arguments" link. The arguments, heard at 10AM and 11AM, are open to the public, but seating is limited. Before a session begins, two lines form on the plaza at the court entrance, often hours before the building opens. One is for those wanting to hear an entire argument, the other for those wanting to observe a session briefly (3–5 minutes). Seating for the first argument begins at 9:30AM; seating for the short-session line begins at 10AM. Be ready for security screening; a coatroom and coin-operated (quarters only) lockers are available for personal belongings. Visitors are also welcome to take a self-guided tour of the building, take in the exhibits, and view a

24-minute film about the supreme court. On days when the court is not sitting, visitors can attend public lectures in the chamber that take place every hour on the half-hour and learn about court procedure and the building's architecture.

TOP PICK!

Bibliophiles must not miss the ★**LIBRARY OF CONGRESS (29)** *(Thomas Jefferson Building, 10 1st St. at Independence Ave.; John Adams Building, 2nd St. and Independence Ave. SE; James Madison Memorial Building bet. 1st/2nd Sts. and Independence Ave. SE, 202-707-8000, www.loc.gov; Jefferson M–Sa 8:30AM–4:30PM; Adams M, W, Th 8:30AM–9:30PM, Tu, F, Sa 8:30AM–5PM; Madison M–F 8:30AM–9:30PM, Sa 8:30AM–5PM).* This is the nation's oldest federal cultural institution, the research arm of

congress, and the largest library in the world. It contains more than 147 million items on 745 miles of shelves, including 34 million books and other printed materials, 3 million recordings, 12 million photographs, 5 million maps, and 64 million manuscripts. The library occupies three buildings on Capitol Hill—its main facility, the copper-domed Thomas Jefferson Building, dating from 1897; the John Adams Building, added in 1938; and the James Madison Memorial Building, which opened in 1981. Established in 1800 with $5,000 appropriated by Congress, the library was housed in the new Capitol (moved from Philadelphia) until 1814, when British troops torched the building, destroying the library. (British Prime Minister Tony Blair apologized to congress for this in 2003.) Thomas Jefferson immediately offered his personal library of more than 6,000 books as a replacement.

Start at the library visitors' center, located at ground level inside the west front entrance of the Jefferson Building. The center provides interactive information kiosks and an award-winning 12-minute film in its visitors' theater. Hour-long tours are offered several times a day Mondays  through Saturdays. The docents must complete a graduate-level training program and their tours are a great way to get acquainted with all this national treasure house has to offer. The library also presents an extraordinary chamber music series which features nationally and internationally known performance ensembles from September through May, as well as an impressive year-round schedule of film screenings, lectures, and themed gallery talks.

On the first floor, you'll find the library's great hall, with its stained-glass skylights and aluminum-leaf-finished beams. On this same floor, in the East Corridor, you'll discover two of the library's great treasures, a Gutenberg Bible and the Giant Bible of Mainz, dating from the 1450s. On the second floor, stop by the visitors' gallery for great views of the domed ceiling that soars 160 feet above the main reading room floor. Stained-glass representations of the seals of 48 states (excluding Alaska and Hawaii) adorn eight semicircular windows; sculptures and paintings abound.

The "Library of Congress Experience" is a must-see. Touch-screen kiosks allow you to examine closely a Jefferson draft of the Declaration of Independence and zero in on the details of the 1507 Waldseemüller map that labels "America" for the first time. You can explore a virtual reality-like version of Jefferson's own library as well. Jefferson arranged his library into three types of knowledge corresponding to Francis Bacon's three faculties of the mind: memory (history), reason (philosophy), and imagination (fine arts).

Stroll the exterior of the Jefferson Building. King Neptune and his court cavort in the famous fountain out front. The first-story window keystones are accented by a series of ethnological heads (33 in all), from Arab to Zulu; they're based on a Smithsonian Institution collection. On the second-story level, busts of nine great men grace the front entrance pavilion: Demosthenes, Emerson, Irving, Goethe, Franklin, Macaulay, Hawthorne, Scott, and Dante.

Anyone 16 and over can be a card-carrying member of the Library of Congress. Bring a driver's license or passport to the Madison building's reader registration room, LM 140 *(ground floor)*. Remember, the Library of Congress is a research library, so all materials must be used on-site.

Arts & Entertainment:

Next to the **Library of Congress (29)** Adams building is the **Folger Shakespeare Library (30)** *(201 E. Capitol St. SE, 202-544-4600, www.folger.edu, M–Sa 10AM–5PM)*, the gift of oil executive Henry Clay Folger. This library holds the first published edition of Shakespeare's comedies, histories, and tragedies, printed in 1623, along with thousands of other books, manuscripts, and items related to the Bard and his work. Inside the building is a reproduction of a 16th-century theater, which stages performances of chamber music, baroque opera, and Shakespearean plays. Amble about the perfectly manicured Elizabethan garden afterward.

East and north of the Capitol Building is the 19th-century Capitol Hill Historic District, known as Jenkins Hill. During the early years of the Republic, few members of Congress established permanent residences in the city. Instead, they chose to live in boardinghouses from which they could walk to the Capitol. Today, the neighborhood is a collection of row houses  from later architectural periods, including Federal, Italianate, Second Empire, Romanesque, Queen Anne, and Classical Revival. It's a feast for the eyes. One of the houses, the **Sewall-Belmont House and Museum (31)** *(144 Constitution Ave. NE 1st/2nd Sts., 202-546-1210, www.sewallbelmont.org)*, was the home of Alice Paul, author of the Equal Rights Amendment. Today, it is a museum dedicated to the early women's rights movement. From there, walk north on First Street to **Union Station (32)** *(50 Massachusetts Ave. NE at 1st St., www.unionstationdc.com, open 24 hours)*. Unlike most railroad stations you've seen, this one is a 1908 Beaux-Arts building restored to the height of its beauty. It houses an international food court, two levels of trendy specialty shops, and from April–October, an outdoor farmer's market featuring organic produce, baked goods, and crafts. It's more than a trans-

portation hub: imagine a presidential inaugural ball here under the 96-foot, gilded waiting room ceiling and you'll get the picture. Just west of the station is the **National Postal Museum (33)** *(2 Massachusetts Ave. at 1st St. NE, 202-633-5555, www.postalmuseum.si.edu, daily 10AM–5:30PM)*. Even if you are not a stamp collector, it is worth a visit. From the vintage airmail planes hanging from the 90-foot-high atrium to stagecoaches, rare

stamps, and interactive exhibits (geared to kids), it's a fun, free philatelic experience for the family. **Barracks Row (34)** *(south of Eastern Market Metro Plaza, on 8th St., 202-544-3188, www.barracksrow.org)* is home to the oldest post of the U.S. Marine Corps, and is also the place where composer John Philip Sousa worked from 1880–1892. If you're here on a Friday evening in summer, you might catch the weekly evening parade and free band performance which takes place in the courtyard of the Marine Corps base *(corner of 8th St. and "Eye," reservations can be made online at http://www.mbw.usmc.mil/RequestReservation.aspx)* beginning at sunset. This area has been revitalized and enlivened by charming shops and new restaurants, and has become one of the hottest areas in DC.

PLACES TO EAT & DRINK
Where to Eat:

Eateries of all varieties abound in this area. From family favorites to power lunches, and from the posh to the unpretentious, you'll find a plethora of dining options. For an established (1960) seafood and meat restaurant where deals are sealed near the Senate side of the Capitol, **The Monocle (35) ($$$)** *(107 D St. NE, 202-546-4488, www.themonocle.com, M–F 11:30AM–10PM, Sa 5PM– 10PM)* is as reliable as it gets. If you prefer a steak and seafood choice with American wine and a view of the Capitol, try **Charlie Palmer Steak (36) ($$$)** *(101 Constitution Ave. NW, 202-547-8100, www.charlie palmer.com, M–F 11:30AM–2:30PM, 5:30PM–10PM, Sa 5PM–10:30PM).* Tucked inside an office building, **Taqueria Nacional (37) ($)** *(400 N. Capitol St. NW, 202-737-7070, www.taquerianacional. com, M–F 7AM–3PM)* is a no-frills taco take-out which offers tacos of all types. They serve breakfast-style tacos with eggs

and coffee in the morning. At lunch the Baja-style fish tacos are especially tasty. For many food choices in one place, **Union Station (32)** offers cafés, casual dining, and restaurants. One of the most distinctive is **B. Smith's (38) ($$-$$$)** *(50 Massachusetts Ave. NE, 202-289-6188, www.bsmith.com, M–Th 11:30AM–9PM, F–Sa 11:30AM–10PM, Su 11AM–9PM),* offering Cajun, Creole, and Southern cuisine in "one of the most beautiful dining rooms in America." In the main hall, street-level **America (39) ($)** *(50 Massachusetts Ave. NE, 202-682-9555, www.arkrestaurants.com, daily 11AM–10PM)* tempts taste buds with a menu of more than 200 traditional dishes inspired by the bounty of America's regional cuisines. Among the choices are Maryland chicken pot pie, pan-fried Virginia ham steak, and Memphis-rubbed ribs. **Market Lunch (40) ($)** *(7th and C Sts. SE, 202-547-8444, Tu–F 7:30AM–2:30PM, Sa 8AM–3PM, Su 9AM–3PM, cash only)* is famous for its breakfast "blubucks"—blueberry/buckwheat pancakes. Lunch? Definitely go for the crab cakes. **Bistro Bis (41) ($$)** *(15 E St. NW, 202-661-2700, www.bistrobis.com, daily 7AM–10AM, 11:30AM–2:30PM, 5:30PM–10:30PM)* in the Hotel George (52) features French food and wine in a modern setting where you're likely to spot senators and house members. For stylish Italian cuisine—such as wood-grilled meats, handmade pasta, and pizza that complements an extensive and well-rounded

wine list, visit **Sonoma (42) ($$)** *(223 Pennsylvania Ave. SE, 202-544-8088, www.sonomadc.com, M–F 11:30AM–2:30PM, M-Th 5PM–10PM, F-Sa 5PM–11PM, Su 5PM–9PM).* Or head over to 8th Street SE, where charming **Montmartre (43) ($$)** *(327 7th St. SE, 202-544-1244, www.montmartredc.com, Tu–F 11:30AM–2:30PM, 5:30PM–10PM, Sa 10:30AM–3PM,*  *5:30PM–10PM, Su 10:30AM–3PM, 5:30PM–9PM)* transports you to Paris with authentic French favorites like braised rabbit and snails in garlic butter. For Indian fare that draws the Capitol Hill crowd, head to **White Tiger (44) ($)** *(301 Massachusetts Ave. NE, 202-546-5900, www.whitetigerdc.com, Su–Th 11:30AM–2:30PM, 5:30PM–10PM, F 11:30AM–2:30PM, 5:30PM–10:30PM, Sa 5:30PM–10:30PM),* featuring a light, Northern Indian menu. Weekday lunch and Sunday brunch buffet prices are good, and tandoor-style meats, curries, and naan are excellent. Treat yourself Teutonic-style at **Café Berlin (45) ($$)** *(322 Massachusetts Ave. NE, 202-543-7656, www.cafeberlindc.com, M–Th 11:30AM–10PM, F–Sa 11:30AM–11PM, Su 10AM–10PM),* where schnitzel, marinated herring, traditional desserts like Black Forest cake, and German beers and wines draw politicians and locals.

Bars & Nightlife:

Mix and mingle at **The Dubliner (46)** *(520 N. Capitol St. NW, 202-737-3773, www.dublinerdc.com,*

Su–Th 11AM–1:30AM, F–Sa 11AM–2:30AM), offering pub favorites like fish and chips and shepherd's pie. Enjoy live Irish music as you quaff your Auld Dubliner Amber Ale. **Hawk & Dove (47)** *(329 Pennsylvania Ave.*

SE, 202-543-3300, www.hawkanddoveonline.com, Su–Th 10AM–2AM, F–Sa 10AM–3AM) is a good pick for well-priced food and drink. It attracts a collegiate and young military crowd, especially at happy hour. **Banana Café & Piano Bar (48)** *(500 8th St. SE, 202-543-5906, www.bananacafedc.com, M–Th 11AM–11:30PM, F–Sa 11AM–12:30AM, Su 11AM–10:30PM)*

makes killer margaritas and authentic Cuban, Puerto Rican, and Mexican dishes. Live piano music is featured seven days a week on the second floor. It's decorated in hues of lime green, tangerine, and pink, accented with local art.

WHERE TO SHOP

Browse away a day at Eastern Market **(49)** *(225 7th/C Sts. SE, 202-544-0083, www.easternmarket-dc.org, closed Mondays, South Hall Tu–F 7AM–7PM, Sa 7AM–6PM, Su 9AM–5PM; Flea Market and Arts and Crafts Market Sa–Su 9AM–6PM; Farmer's Market Sa–Su 7AM–4PM).* Housed in a 19th-century brick building designed by Adolf Cluss, the market is the centerpiece of this old-fashioned neighborhood. Try the South Hall, a public market, for fresh produce, flowers, bakery items, poultry, and cheese. The North Hall is an arts and community center. On weekends, there's a flea market filled with antiques and crafts. The "farmer's line" is held on weekends, too. Farmers bring their wares from Maryland, Virginia, Pennsylvania, and West Virginia—some from families who have been coming since the market was built. In Barracks Row, **Groovy DC (50)** *(428 8th St. SE, 202-544-6633, www.groovydc.com, M–Sa 10AM–6PM, Su noon–5PM)* has lots of fun stuff for the kitsch–inclined, including greeting cards, candles, and seasonal gift items.

Otherwise, a trip to **East Hall (51)** at **Union Station (32)** *(50 Massachusetts Ave. NE, 202-289-1908, www.unionstationdc.com, M–Sa 10AM–9PM, Su noon–6PM)* will yield great finds: **Aurea** for high-end jewelry with an international flair, local designer **Heydari** for chic women's fashions, and **America's Spirit** for DC trinkets. You'll shop your way around the world.

If you like being in the center of activity, this area is for you. Most hotels are clustered between Capitol Hill and **Union Station (32)** to the north, near the Senate side. If you prefer contemporary to conventional, stay at hip **Hotel George (52) ($$-$$$)** *(15 E St. NW, 202-347-4200 or 800-576-8331, www.hotel george.com)*, a boutique hotel with stylish, sleek, yet comfortable rooms. For traditional on a grand scale, choose the **Hyatt Regency Washington on Capitol Hill (53) ($$-$$$)** *(400 New Jersey Ave. NW, 202-737-1234, www.hyattregencywashington.com)*, with its five-story atrium. At the **Phoenix Park Hotel (54) ($$-$$$)** *(520 N. Capitol St. NW, 202-638-6900, www.phoenixparkhotel.com)*, Celtic charm abounds. For a different atmosphere on the House side, **Capitol Hill Suites (55) ($-$$)** *(200 C St. SE, 202-543-6000, www.capitolhillsuites.com)*, located on a quiet residential street, offers 152 rooms; its patrons include those working at the Library of Congress. Rates are better on the weekends, when life on the Hill slows down. The **Liaison Capitol Hill (56) ($$)** *(415 New Jersey Ave. NW, 202-638-1616, www.affinia.com/liaison)*, is upscale chic, with well-appointed rooms and a seasonal rooftop

pool and sundeck. The Washington Court Hotel on Capitol Hill (57) ($$$) *(525 New Jersey Ave. NW, 202-628-2100 or 800-321-3010, www.washingtoncourt hotel.com)* has a refined elegance and is known for its exceptional service.

In Washington, DC, politics dominate even the most casual conversations.

—*Armstrong Williams*

chapter 3

GEORGETOWN AND
WASHINGTON HARBOUR

FOGGY BOTTOM

Places to See:

1. Old Stone House
2. Chesapeake and Ohio (C&O) Canal
3. Washington Harbour
4. Tudor Place Historic House and Garden
5. Dumbarton Oaks and Gardens
6. Dumbarton House
7. 3260 N Street
8. 3307 N Street
9. 3038 N Street
10. Georgetown University
11. Francis Scott Key Memorial Park
59. Federal Reserve Board Building
60. National Academy of Sciences (NAS)
61. Albert Einstein Memorial
62. U.S. Department of State Diplomatic Reception Rooms
63. George Washington University
64. Lisner Auditorium
65. International Monetary Fund Center
66. World Bank
67. U.S. Department of Interior Museum
68. John F. Kennedy Center for the Performing Arts
69. Thompson Boat Center
70. B'nai B'rith Klutznick National Jewish Museum Collection and Gallery
71. Arts Club of Washington

Places to Eat & Drink:

12. La Chaumière
13. 1789 Restaurant
14. Neyla
15. Filomena Ristorante
16. Café Milano
17. Morton's of Chicago
18. Peacock Café
19. Bangkok Bistro
20. Café Bonaparte
21. Café La Ruche
22. Clyde's of Georgetown
23. Michel Richard Citronelle
24. Bourbon Steak

Where to Shop:

Where to Stay:

● ● *to Foggy Bottom-GWU*

• SNAPSHOT •

Georgetown is one of the liveliest and most historic neighborhoods in the Washington, DC area. It retains its cachet as the separate town it once was in 1751, when it was named in honor of King George II. Because of its desirability as a port, the U.S. Congress decided to annex it to the city of Washington in 1871. Situated on the Potomac River, Georgetown developed as a commercial and industrial hub around Washington Harbour, prospering from shipping and tobacco. Through the years, prosperity has ebbed and flowed, but Georgetown kept its reputation, and, so far, has managed to keep the Metro out of the neighborhood. It is connected by numerous Metro buses to the closest Metro stop, Foggy Bottom, and by the DC Circulator bus *(see page 8)* to Union Station and the Washington Convention Center. What makes Georgetown great is its location on the Potomac, and its distinctive charm and character, from its tree-lined streets and plentiful restaurants, taverns, shops, and hotels, to its renowned residents and historic archi-

89

tecture, including Georgian, Federal, and Classical Revival styles.

PLACES TO SEE
Landmarks:

M Street, running east to west, and Wisconsin Avenue, running northwest to south, are the main thoroughfares in Georgetown. Some major landmarks date back to the mid-1700s, transporting you to another era. The **Old Stone House (1)** *(3051 M St. NW, 202-426-6851, www. nps.gov/rocr/olst, daily noon–5PM)* is a reminder of Georgetown's 18th-century past. Dating to 1765, it's one of the oldest structures in Washington and offers a superb glimpse into colonial life. Another way to experience Georgetown's past is to stroll the towpath once used by mules or ride a canal barge along the **Chesapeake and Ohio (C&O) Canal (2)** *(National Park Service Visitor Center, 1057 Thomas Jefferson St. NW, just south of M St., 202-653-5190, www.nps.gov/choh; visitor center Apr–Oct W–Su 9:30AM–4:30PM, call for barge ride times. visitor center only Nov–Mar, Sa–Su 10AM–4PM)*. Period-costumed guides lead mule-drawn canal boat rides through Georgetown's old warehouse district—a

fun way to relax and learn! After walking south to the bottom of Thomas Jefferson Street, catch the view of **Washington Harbour (3)** *(3000 K St. NW)* from the boardwalk, where the central fountain court sends sprays of water up against the backdrop of the Potomac. Visit at sunset or twilight for a romantic rendezvous. Head north of M Street, the main thoroughfare, and follow 31st Street north. The real Georgetown lies off the major arteries, where Federal-era mansions and town houses abound, including those made famous by President John F. Kennedy and his family. These are now private residences. **Tudor Place Historic House and Garden (4)** *(1644 31st St. NW, 202-965-0400, www.tudorplace.org, tours Tu–Sa 10AM–4PM, Su noon–4PM, on the hour until 1 hour before closing, closed Jan)*, once the home of Martha Washington's granddaughter, Martha Custis Peter, is a lovely example of Federal architecture and features a domed roof portico.

Peter, who purchased the land with a legacy from her grandmother, planted some of the property's boxwoods in the five-acre garden herself. A few minutes farther north, you'll find **Dumbarton Oaks and Gardens (5)** *(1703 32nd St. NW, 202-339-6401, www.doaks.org; gardens Mar 15–Oct 31 Tu–Su 2PM–6PM, Nov 1–Mar 14 Tu–Su 2PM–5PM; museum Tu–Su 2PM–5PM)*, a 10-acre garden of formal terraces, garden rooms, and naturalistic areas; Dumbarton Oaks, an 1801 Federal mansion owned by Harvard University, maintains collections of Byzantine and pre-Columbian art and rare books. A few blocks southeast is **Dumbarton House (6)** *(2715 Q St., 27th/28th Sts. NW, 202-337-2288, www.dumbartonhouse.org, mid-March to mid-Dec Tu–F 10AM–4PM, Sa–Su 11AM–3PM, mid-Dec to mid-Mar Tu–Su 11AM–3PM)*, another Federal-style residence. If period furniture and decorative arts are your fancy, take a docent-led tour. If you're a Kennedy buff, wander south to N Street to see some of their family homes. JFK lived in **3260 N Street (7)** when he began his senate career. He purchased **3307 N Street (8)** for Jackie after the birth of their daughter Caroline in 1957. Jackie, Caroline, and John Jr. lived in **3038 N Street (9)** temporarily after JFK's assassination. Georgetown is also the home of **Georgetown University (10)** *(37th/O Sts. NW, 202-687-0100, www.georgetown.edu)*, the oldest Catholic university in the U.S. The tower of its Healy Hall, a Romanesque Revival structure, features prominently in the city's skyline. For a bit of green, find solace at the **Francis Scott Key Memorial Park (11)** *(M St., 34th St./Key Bridge)*.

PLACES TO EAT & DRINK
Where to Eat:

Georgetown has more restaurants than almost any Washington, DC neighborhood. One of its best dining spots for food, ambience, and service is **La Chaumière (12) ($$)** *(2813 M St. NW, 202-338-1784, www. lachaumieredc.com, M–F 11:30AM–2:30PM, 5:30PM–10:30PM, Sa 5:30PM–10:30PM)*, an award-winning French country "inn" that draws a crowd even on weekday nights. Leave room for the chocolate or Grand Marnier soufflé, a house specialty. A good choice for formal occasions is **1789 Restaurant (13) ($$$)** *(1226 36th St. at Prospect St., 202-965-1789, www.1789 restaurant.com, M–Th 6PM–10PM, F 6PM–11PM, Sa 5:30PM–11PM, Su 5:30PM–10PM)*, located in a renovated Federal house near the university. The signature dish?

Rack of lamb with creamy feta potatoes. For Lebanese cuisine in an exotic atmosphere—with pillows, muted lighting, and international music—choose **Neyla (14) ($$)** *(3206 N St. NW, 202-333-6353, www.neyla.com, M–Th 5PM–10:30PM, F–Sa 5PM–11:30PM, Su 3PM–9:30PM, bar hours later)*. The menu features small plates, designed for sharing. Try the beet and fennel salad with goat cheese, grilled halloumi cheese with watermelon, or *pommes frites* with cilantro. Celebrities, politicos, and tourists alike gather at **Filomena Ristorante (15) ($$–$$$)** *(1063 Wisconsin Ave. NW, 202-338-8800, www.filomenadc.com, daily 11:30AM–11PM)* to watch the "mamas" make homemade pasta in

the front window. For other tempting venues, head to Prospect Street, one block north of M Street and one block west of Wisconsin. **Café Milano (16) ($$$)** *(3251 Prospect St. NW, 202-333-6183, www.cafemilano. net, daily 11:30AM–4PM, W–Sa 4PM–midnight, Su–Tu 4PM–11PM)* offers new Italian food and a high level of service. **Morton's of Chicago (17) ($$$)** *(3251 Prospect St. NW, 202-342-6258, www.mortons.com, M–Sa 5PM–11PM, Su 5PM–10PM)* serves steak in a "power" atmosphere. **Peacock Café (18) ($$)** *(3251 Prospect St. NW,*

202-625-2740, www.peacockcafe.com, M–Th 11AM–10PM, F 11AM–11PM, Sa 9AM–11PM, Su 9AM–10PM) provides an eclectic menu. Order the figs and gorgonzola over grilled brioche for a starter. Diners give kudos for the grilled lamb steak with tomato basil relish.

For Asian and Thai food in a casual setting, try **Bangkok Bistro (19) ($)** *(3251 Prospect St. NW, 202-337-2424, www.bangkokbistrodc.com, Su–Th 11:30AM–10:30PM, F–Sa 11:30AM–11:30PM)*. It's a student favorite for Pad Thai and curries at value prices. Further up Wisconsin Avenue, **Café Bonaparte (20) ($-$$)** *(1522 Wisconsin Ave. NW, P St./Volta Pl., 202-333-8830, www.cafebonaparte. com, M–Th 10AM–11PM, F–Sa 10AM–midnight, Su 9AM–10PM)*, a tiny *crêperie*, coffee shop, and bar, is as good as it is authentic. Its Moulin Rouge crêpe, caramelized peaches with vanilla ice cream and chocolate-and-melba sauce, is scrumptious. For French bistro fare and delectable pastries, try **Café La Ruche (21) ($)** *(1039 31st St. NW, 202-965-2684, www.cafelaruche.com, M–Th 11:30AM–midnight, F 11:30AM–1AM, Sa 10AM– 1AM, Su 10AM–midnight)*, "a bit of Paris on the Potomac." It's a Georgetown institution. A reliable place for burgers and other informal fare is **Clyde's of Georgetown (22) ($)** *(3236 M St. NW, 202-333-9180, www.clydes.com, M–Th 11:30AM–midnight, F 11:30AM– 1AM, Sa 10AM–1AM, Su 9AM–midnight)*, this unique local chain's original location. The song "Afternoon Delight" was inspired by its late-afternoon appetizer menu; the gold record hangs in the restaurant. For a special evening out featuring California/French cuisine, **Michel Richard Citronelle (23) ($$$)** *(3000 M St. NW, 202-625-2150, www.citronelledc.com, Tu–Th 6PM–10PM, F–Sa 6PM–*

10:30PM) is the ticket. Chef Richard offers inventive twists on lamb, rabbit, lobster, and venison. A main dining room "mood wall"

constantly changes color. Michael Mina's **Bourbon Steak (24) ($$$)** *(2800 Pennsylvania Ave. NW, 202-944-2026, www.michaelmina.net, M–Th 11AM–midnight, F–Sa 11AM–1AM, Su 6PM–10PM)*, located at the Four Seasons Hotel (53), skews to contemporary American. The steaks are fantastic, the atmosphere is clubby-swank, and the service is over the top. Another top spot is **Fahrenheit (25) ($$$)** *(Ritz-Carlton, 3100 South St. NW, 202-912-4110, www.ritz carlton.com, M 6:30AM–2:30PM, Tu–Th 6:30AM–2:30PM, 6PM–10PM, F 6:30AM–2:30PM, 6PM–11PM, Sa 7AM–2:30PM, 6PM–11PM, Su 7AM–2:30PM)*, where the contemporary decor sets the stage for a special evening. **Five Guys**

(26) ($) *(1335 Wisconsin Ave. NW, 202-337-0400, www.fiveguys.com, Su–Th 11AM–11PM, F–Sa 11AM–4AM)*, local hamburger joint gone national, makes each hamburger to order. A New England fish shanty in DC? **The Tackle Box (27) ($)** *(3245 M St. NW, 202-337-8269, www.tackleboxrestaurant.com, Su–Th 11AM–11PM, F–Su 11AM–1AM)* is picnic-table casual. The "Maine meal" offers a choice of fish, two sides, one sauce, and is a great deal. You'll feel good eating here, too—this is strictly sustainable fin fare. The pizza is heavenly at **Pizzeria Paradiso (28) ($)** *(3282 M St. NW, 202-337-1245, www.eatyourpizza.com, M–Th 11:30AM–11PM, F–Sa 11:30AM–midnight, Su noon–10PM)*. Mix with Georgetown students at **The Tombs (29) ($)** *(1226 36th St. NW, 202-337-6668, www. tombs.com, M–Th 11:30AM–1:15AM, F 11:30AM–2:15AM,*

Sa 11AM–2:15AM, Su 9:30AM–1:15AM) for soup, sandwiches, and burgers. For fresh seafood and Potomac views, try **Tony & Joe's Seafood Place (30) ($$)** *(3000 K St. NW, 202-944-4545, www.tonyandjoes.com, Su–Th 11AM–10PM, F–Sa 11AM–midnight)* on Washington Harbour.

Bars & Nightlife:

Trendy **Sequoia (31)** *(3000 K St. NW, 202-944-4200, www.arkrestaurants.com, M–Th 11:30AM–11PM, F–Sa 11:30AM–11PM, Su 10:30AM–11PM)* has an enormous bar on the ground floor and a multilevel terrace with outdoor tables; it also boasts great views and a varied American menu. It's a popular spot on spring and summer evenings. Georgetown's famous **Blues Alley (32)** *(1073 Wisconsin Ave. NW, south of M St., 202-337-4141, www.bluesalley.com, daily 6PM–12:30AM)* jazz and supper club (Cajun cuisine is featured) features artists like Tony Bennett, Wynton Marsalis, and  Nancy Wilson. Hobnob with the power elite at **Degrees Bar & Lounge (33)** *(Ritz-Carlton, 3100 South St. NW, 202-912-4100, www.ritzcarlton.com, Su–Tu 2:30PM–11PM, W–Th 2:30PM–11:30PM, F–Sa 2:30PM–1:30AM)* in the Ritz-Carlton (57). The lounge exudes 1940s style. Try the "Fahrenheit Five" martini, the hotel's specialty. Subterranean **L2 Lounge (34)** *(3315 Cady's Alley NW, 202-956-2001, www.l2lounge.com, W 6PM–2AM, Th 9PM–2AM, F–Sa 9PM–3AM)* is a glam VIP night spot (with a strictly enforced dress code). **Martin's Tavern (35)** *(1264 Wisconsin Ave., north of M St., 202-333-7370,* *www.martins-tavern.com, M–Th 11AM–1:30AM, F 11AM–2:30AM, Sa 9AM–2:30AM, Su 9AM–1:30AM)* has been around since 1933, attracting presidents, locals, and tourists to its famous mahogany bar.

WHERE TO SHOP

Georgetown is a mix of home furnishing stores, boutiques, specialty shops, and ice cream and sweets emporiums. Check out **Appalachian Spring (36)** *(1415 Wisconsin Ave. NW, 202-337-5780, www.appalachianspring.com M–Sa 10AM–6PM, Su noon–6PM)* for quilts, blown glass, wood sculptures, colorful

pottery, and jewelry. The **Cady's Alley Design District (37)** *(3318 M St. NW, www.cadysalley.com, individual store hours vary)* houses more than a dozen international and local home furnishing retailers, such as **Poggenpohl** and **Thos. Moser**, in one very cool industrial space. For antique prints and maps, browse **The Old Print Gallery (38)** *(1220 31st St. NW, 202-965-1818, www.oldprintgallery.com, Tu–Sa 10AM–5:30PM)*. For exquisite European fashions for baby and kids, parents (and doting grandparents) flock to **Piccolo Piggies (39)** *(1533 Wisconsin Ave. NW, 202-333-0123, www.piccolo-piggies.com, M–Sa 10AM–6PM, Su 11:30AM–5PM)*. **A Mano, Ltd. (40)** *(1677 Wisconsin Ave. NW, 202-298-7200, www.amano.bz, M–Sa 10AM–6PM, Su noon–5PM)*— "a mano" means "by hand"—carries French and Italian hand-painted tableware, crystal, china, and linens. **Sassanova (41)** *(1641 Wisconsin Ave. NW, 202-471-4400, www.sassanovadc.blogspot.com, M–W, F–Sa 10AM–6PM, Th*

10AM–7PM, Su noon–5PM) stocks high-end shoes, handbags, and jewelry. Dangerous! **The Phoenix (42)** *(1514 Wisconsin Ave. NW, 202-338-4404, www.thephoenixdc.com, M–Sa 10AM–6PM, winter Su noon–5PM, summer Su 1PM–6PM)* has been selling contemporary clothes like Eileen Fisher and handcrafted gift items from around the world since 1955. For shoes, eyewear, handbags, and accessories from Marc Jacobs, Moschino, and Versace, **Focus (43)** *(1330 Wisconsin Ave. NW, 202-337-8969, www.fashionby focus.com, M–Sa 11AM–8PM, Su noon–6PM)* is a good bet. The **Opportunity Shop of the Christ Child Society (44)** *(1427 Wisconsin Ave. NW, 202-333-6635, http://www.christchild dc.org/opportunity_shop/index.aspx, Sep–June M–Sa 10AM– 5PM, Su noon–4PM, July–Aug M noon–4PM, Tu–Sa 10AM–5PM)* is a neighborhood institution. Consignment goods—silver, furniture and more—are attractively displayed. Check out the **Shops at Georgetown Park**, such as **Intermix (45)** *(3222 M St. NW, 202-298-5577, www.intermixonline.com, M–Sa 10AM–9PM, Su noon–6PM),* a Madison Avenue-based retailer of trendy yet wearable women's fashions. Wander the four-story Victorian-style mall for other name-brand shops. Waits of up to an hour are not uncommon, but a treat from **Georgetown Cupcake (46)** *(3301 M St. NW, 202-333-8448, www.georgetown cupcake.com, M–Sa 10AM–9PM, Su 11AM–7PM)* is so worth it. Their signature cupcake—the red velvet—is highly recommended. **Leonidas Chocolates (47)** *(1531 Wisconsin Ave. NW, 202-944-1898, www.leonidasdc.com, Su–M 11AM– 5PM, Tu–Sa 10AM–6PM)* dispenses decadent Belgian chocolates and confectionaries. Famed New York City-based food emporium **Dean & Deluca (48)** *(3276 M St. NW, 202-342-*

2500, www.deandeluca.com, M–Su 9AM–
8PM) is packed with epicurean delights.
If you're looking for antiques and art,
browse the shops near the **Four Seasons
Hotel (53)**, such as **Gallery Lareuse (49)**
*(2820 Pennsylvania Ave. NW, 202-333-
1506, www.galerielareuse.com, Tu–Sa 11AM–7PM)*, showcasing works by Europeans and Americans. For Lalique, Gallé,
Tiffany, and Steuben, visit **Cherub Antiques Gallery (50)**
*(2918 M St. NW, 202-337-2224, M–Sa 11AM–6PM, Su
noon–5PM)*. **Michael Getz Antiques (51)** *(2918 M St. NW,
202-338-3811, M–Sa 11AM–6PM, Su noon–5PM)* shares the
town house space and specializes in American, British, and
Continental silver. Take a trip down memory lane at
Animation Sensations (52) *(2909-1/2 M St. NW, 202-338-
1097, www.animationsensations.com, M–F 10AM–6PM, Sa
11AM–6PM, Su noon–5PM)*, where Disney and Warner
Brothers animation art cels, drawings, and production
backgrounds are available to buy or browse.

WHERE TO STAY

Be pampered at the **Four Seasons Hotel (53) ($$$)**
*(2800 Pennsylvania Ave. NW, 202-342-0444, www.
fourseasons.com)* on the eastern edge of Georgetown. For a

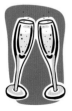

"see and be seen" experience, stop at
Bourbon Steak Lounge *(also see page 95)*
in the lobby for drinks. Diplomats and
film stars choose the elegant **Georgetown
Inn (54) ($$-$$$)** *(1310 Wisconsin Ave.
NW, 202-333-8900 or 888-587-2388,
www.georgetowninn.com)*, famed for its

anticipate-your-every-need service. For quaint European style, stay at the Inn's sister property, **The Latham Hotel (55)** **($$-$$$)** *(3000 M St. NW, 202-726-5000 or 1-800-368-5922, www.thelatham.com)*, overlooking the C&O Canal. For the comforts of home and convenience to both Georgetown and George Washington Universities, stay at **Georgetown Suites (56) ($$-$$$)** *(1111 30th St. NW and 1000 29th St. NW, 202-298-7800 or 800-348-7203, www.georgetownsuites.com)*; fully equipped kitchens and complimentary breakfast are included. An excellent value. The luxurious **Ritz-Carlton (57) ($$$)** *(3100 South St. NW, 202-912-4100 or 1-800-241-3333, www.ritzcarlton.com)* is located in a historic 1932 incinerator building with a smokestack. Its lobby lounge fireplace warms the red brick interior in winter. For reasonable rates, book the **Holiday Inn Georgetown (58) ($$)** *(2101 Wisconsin Ave. NW, 202-338-3120, www.higeorgetown.com)*, offering traditional accommodations and dining.

⬤ ⬤ *to Foggy Bottom-GWU, or Farragut West*

• SNAPSHOT •

Foggy Bottom, also known as the West End, is a stately neighborhood between Georgetown and Lafayette Square. It's home to the U.S. Department of State, part of the National Academy of Sciences, the International Monetary Fund, Watergate, the Federal Reserve, the John F. Kennedy Center for the Performing Arts, George Washington University, and some of the best restaurants in the Capital City. The residential neighborhood near the Foggy Bottom Metro stop is lined with charming 19th-century town houses, former homes of the area's earliest residents: working-class Irish, Germans, and African Americans. Smoke from the factories in which they worked produced continual fog along the Potomac waterfront here, hence the name "Foggy Bottom." Today, expensive condominiums have sprung up in the neighborhood, and a number of high-end hotels dot the area. The distance to points of interest can be a bit far from the Foggy Bottom Metro stop. You might want to rely on buses from Georgetown or Lafayette Square instead, as several key places are clustered together along Constitution Avenue and west of 18th Street.

PLACES TO SEE
Landmarks:

Start by walking west on Constitution to the **Federal Reserve Board Building (59)** *(Constitution Ave. NW, 20th/21st Sts., 202-452-3778, www.federalreserve.gov, art exhibit hours M–F 10AM–3PM)*, a commanding marble building that houses the watchdogs of the U.S. economy. Tours are no longer offered to the general public, but visitors are invited to view the Fed's changing art exhibits by appointment. Next door is the **National Academy of Sciences (NAS) (60)** *(2101 Constitution Ave. NW, 202-334-2436, www.nationalacademies.org/arts, M–F 9AM–5PM; enter at 2100 C St. NW)*, the organization that advises congress of breakthroughs and studies in medicine, science, and engineering. Free monthly concerts by internationally renowned musicians take place in the auditorium on Sunday afternoons. There are also two

galleries that display fascinating science-related art. In the southwest corner of the Academy grounds, you'll find the **Albert Einstein Memorial (61)** *(2101 Constitution Ave. NW)*. The 12-foot bronze statue portrays the scientist seated, holding a sheet of mathematical equations. A 28-foot celestial map is at his feet. One block north on C Street, the **U.S. Department of State Diplomatic Reception Rooms (62)** *(2201 C St. NW, 202-647-3241, http://receptiontours.state.gov, tours M–F at 9:30AM, 10:30AM, and 2:45PM)* houses a superb collection of 18th-century American paintings, furniture, and decorative arts, including pieces by Revere and

Chippendale. Reservations are required 90 days in advance for this 45-minute fine arts tour. **George Washington University (63)** *(2121 I St. NW, 202-994-1000, www.gwu.edu)* was founded in 1822; its campus is filled with Colonial Revival architecture. Also located on campus is **Lisner Auditorium (64)** *(730 21st St. NW, 202-994-6800, www.lisner.org)*. The public is invited to its music, dance, and theater programs. Nearby is the **International Monetary Fund Center (65)** *(720 19th St. NW, 202-623-7000)*. The nearby **World Bank (66)** *(1818 H St. NW, 202-473-1000, www.worldbank.org)* provides assistance to developing countries. To learn more or to purchase unique gifts and books, visit the adjacent **J Building Info Shop** *(701 18th St. NW, 202-458-4500, M–F 9:30AM–5:30PM)*.

Arts & Entertainment:

If wildlife, Native American affairs, land management, and geology interest you, you might enjoy the dioramas and murals of the **U.S. Department of Interior Museum (67)** *(1849 C St. NW, 202-208-4743, www.doi.gov/interior museum; museum is closed for renovations but offering limited public programs, call for info)*. Though this neighborhood is dominated by university and federal buildings, it also boasts a world-class arts venue, the **John F. Kennedy Center for the Performing Arts (68)** *(2700 F St. NW, 202-467-4600, www.kennedy-center.org, daily 10AM–11PM, tours M–F 10AM–5PM, Sa–Su 10AM–1PM)*, where you can enjoy a concert, play, opera, or dance performance. A free Kennedy Center Show Shuttle runs between the Center and the Foggy Bottom Metro stop. Free daily perform-

ances take place at the **Millennium Stage** nearly every evening at 6PM. The range of performances is incredible, often featuring young, up-and-coming national and international artists. Many of the Kennedy Center furnishings were donated by other countries, including the impressive Orrefors crystal chandeliers from Sweden in the foyer and the white Carrara marble from Italy. Stroll the landscaped terrace overlooking the Potomac before or after. For outdoor diversion, **Thompson Boat Center (69)** *(2900 Virginia Ave. NW, 202-333-9543, www.thompson boatcenter.com, spring/summer M–Sa 6AM–8PM, Su 7AM–7PM, Fall 8AM–5PM)* rents canoes, sailboats, rowing shells, and kayaks, and offers group lessons as well. Paddle along the Potomac and dock over at Roosevelt Island (see page 203). It's within easy rowing distance and a nice way to get away from it all. If you're a land-lubber, choose an all-terrain bike instead. In this neighborhood you will also find the infamous **Watergate Complex**, practically a city within a city, with offices, apartments, shops, and restaurants. To learn about the history and contributions of the Jewish people, visit the **B'nai B'rith Klutznick National Jewish Museum Collection and Gallery (70)** *(2020 K St. NW, 202-857-6647, www.bnaibrith.org/ prog_serv/museum.cfm, 9AM–5PM by advance reservation only)*. It's the home of George Washington's 1790 letter to the Touro Synagogue in Rhode Island, pledging "to bigotry no sanction." Another cultural venue is the **Arts Club of Washington (71)** *(2017 I St. NW, 202-331-7282, www.arts clubofwashington.org, Tu–F 10AM–5PM, Sa 10AM–2PM)*, the oldest nonprofit arts organization in the city. It offers free concerts, seminars, and literary events in an 1805 Georgian-style house, once the home of president James Monroe.

PLACES TO EAT & DRINK
Where to Eat:

It's exciting to be able to choose from so many top-notch restaurants in one place. But they're all popular; be sure to plan ahead and reserve early if there's a special place you want to experience while you're here. Among the best is **Marcel's (72) ($$$)** *(2401 Pennsylvania Ave. NW, 202-296-1166, www.marcelsdc.com, M–Th 5:30PM–10PM, F–Sa 5:30PM–11PM, Su 5:30PM–9:30PM)*, serving French cuisine with a Flemish accent. A pre-theater menu includes complimentary limo service to and from the Kennedy Center. Return afterward for dessert and jazz piano in the wine bar. Another DC favorite is **Kinkead's (73) ($$-$$$)** *(2000 Pennsylvania Ave. NW, 202-296-7700, www.kinkead.com, M–Th 11:30AM–2:30PM, 5:30PM–10PM, F 11:30AM–2:30PM, 5:30PM–10:30PM, Sa 5:30PM–10:30PM, Su 5:30PM–10PM)*, where the food is tops and the atmosphere convivial. The emphasis is on seafood here—go for the pepita-crusted salmon. At **Greek Deli & Catering (74) ($)** *(1120 19th St. NW, 202-296-2111, www.greekdelidc.com, M–F 7AM–4PM)* long lines queue up every weekday for the best souvlaki, gyros, and moussaka in town. With red-and-white checkered tablecloths and Chianti bottle candles,

Famous Luigi's (75) ($$) *(1132 19th St. NW, 202-331-7574, www.famousluigis.com, M–Sa 11AM–midnight, Su noon–midnight)* has been serving excellent old-school family-style Italian cuisine since 1943. For a pre-concert or pre-theater meal, **DISH (76) ($$)** *(924 25th St. NW, I/K Sts., 202-338-8707, www.theriverinn.com, M–Sa 7AM–10AM, 11:30AM–2PM, 5PM–9PM)* at the River Inn offers warm ambience, complete with a fireplace and American classics.

Roof Terrace Restaurant and Bar (77) ($$-$$$) *(2700 F St. NW, 202-416-8555, www.kennedy-center.org, Su–W 5PM–8PM, Th–Sa 5PM–9PM, Su brunch 11:30AM–2:30PM, shuttle from Foggy Bottom Metro stop every 15 min.)* offers an unforgettable dining experience that includes modern American food and a panoramic view of the Potomac. Farm fresh flavor comes to DC at **Blue Duck Tavern (78)** *(24th and M Sts., 202-419-6755, www.blueducktavern.com, M–F 6:30AM–10:30AM, 11:30AM–2:30PM, 5:30PM–10:30PM, Sa–Su 11AM–2:30AM, 5:30PM–10:30PM)* serving gourmet comfort food that celebrates Mid-Atlantic culinary traditions. Main course hits include braised cod with white bean cassoulet or duck breast with huckleberries. The **Rivers at the Watergate (79) ($$-$$$)** *(Watergate complex, 600 New Hampshire Ave. NW, 202-333-1600, www.rivers dc.com, M 11:30AM–9PM, Tu–Th 11:30AM–11PM, F 11AM–midnight, Sa 5PM–midnight)* is a hot spot for before the theater, after sightseeing, or for a simple lunch downtown—with a million-dollar view. **Nooshi (80) ($)** *(1120 19th St. NW, 202-293-3138, www.nooshidc.com, M–Sa*

11:30AM–11PM, Su 5PM–10PM) has slurpilicious noodles of every type, sit-down service, and reasonable prices. Sushi too!

Bars & Nightlife:

Sip cocktails in a leather easy chair at **The Bar (81)**, West End Ritz Carlton, *(1150 22nd St. on M St. NW, 202-835-0500, or 800-241-3333, www.ritz carlton.com, M–Th 11:30AM–10PM, F 11:30AM–11PM, Sa–Su 5:30PM–11PM)*. The **Science Club (82)** *(1136 19th St. NW, 202-775-0747, www.scienceclub dc.com, M–Th 5PM–2AM, F–Sa 5PM–3AM)* features a vegetarian menu in the form of the Periodic Table, has a lively happy hour scene, and a nightly DJ. Miss your favorite New York sports teams? Watch them at **The 51st State Tavern (83)** *(2512 L St. NW, 202-625-2444, www.51ststate tavern.com, Su–Th 4PM–2AM, F–Sa 4PM–3AM)*; it boasts several screens, including a 60-inch plasma TV, as well as antique bars on two floors, Internet jukeboxes, and a pool table.

WHERE TO SHOP

This area is not known for its shopping, as Georgetown is, but there are some finds here. **Chocolate Moose (84)** *(1743 L St. NW, 202-463-0992, www.chocolatemoose dc.com, M–Sa 10AM–6PM)* is serious fun—an overstuffed store featuring pop-culture goods, funky housewares, and retro toys. The **Indian Craft Shop (85)** *(1849 C St. NW, 202-208-4056, www.indiancraftshop.com, M–F 8:30AM–4:30PM, 3rd Sa of the month 10AM–4PM)*, located within the **U.S. Department of Interior Museum (67)**, sells authentic Native American jewelry, pottery, and hand-woven rugs. It is open even though the museum is under renovation.

WHERE TO STAY

For luxury, elegance, and a state-of-the-art health club, **The Fairmont Washington, DC (86)** **($$$)** *(2401 M St. NW, 202-429-2400 or 800-441-1414, www. fairmont.com/washington)* is a great choice. The **Park Hyatt Washington (87)** **($$$)** *(24th and M Sts. NW, 202-789-1234 or 800-778-7477, www.parkhyatt washington.com)*, captures modern style with contemporary lighting, wooden blinds, and authentic folk art. The **Melrose Hotel (88)** **($$-$$$)** *(2430 Pennsylvania Ave. NW, 202-955-6400 or 800-MEL-ROSE, www.melrosehoteldc.com)* is a good value for

the area and has rooms and suites that are among the largest in the city, as well as Wi-Fi. A plush boutique hotel, **The River Inn (89)** **($$-$$$)** *(924 25th St. NW, 202-337-7600 or 888-874-0100, www.theriverinn.com)* offers cozy comfort. The **West End Ritz-Carlton, Washington, DC (90)** **($$$)** *(1150 22nd St. on M St. NW, 202-835-0500 or 800-241-3333, www.ritz carlton.com)* has it all—goosedown pillows, marble tubs, a spa, and afternoon tea. **One Washington Circle Hotel (91)** **($-$$)** *(One Washington Circle, NW, 202-872-1680, 800-424-9671, www.thecirclehotel.com)* offers pleasant, spacious suites, a seasonal outdoor pool, and an unbeatable location. The extra-spacious two-room suites at the Embassy Suites Washington DC (92) ($$) *(1250 22nd St. NW, 202-857-3388, www.embassy suites.com)* cost no more than a single room elsewhere. This Embassy Suites location has an indoor pool, and room rates include happy hour drinks and snacks as well as a buffet breakfast.

chapter 4

DOWNTOWN

CHINATOWN

PENN QUARTER

DOWNTOWN
CHINATOWN
PENN QUARTER

Places to See:

1. Ronald Reagan Building and International Trade Center
2. The Old Post Office Pavilion
3. National Archives Building
4. Federal Trade Commission
5. Canadian Embassy
6. U.S. Navy Memorial and Navy Heritage Center
7. J. Edgar Hoover Building
8. Martin Luther King, Jr. Memorial Library
9. Newseum
10. Madame Tussaud's
11. National Theatre
12. Warner Theatre
13. Ford's Theatre
14. Lansburgh Theatre
15. Sidney Harman Hall
16. Woolly Mammoth Theatre Company
17. The Capitol Steps
18. International Spy Museum
19. National Portrait Gallery/Smithsonian American Art Museum
20. Gallery at Flashpoint
21. Civilian Art Projects
22. Touchstone Gallery
23. Edison Place Gallery
24. National Museum of Crime & Punishment
25. National Geographic Museum at Explorers Hall
26. National Museum of Women in the Arts
27. Sixth and I Synagogue
28. Goethe-Institut
29. Lillian & Albert Small Jewish Museum
30. Verizon Center
31. National Building Museum
32. Marian Koshland Science Museum

Places to Eat & Drink:

33. Againn DC
34. Capital Grille
35. Café Atlantico
36. Rasika

DOWNTOWN
CHINATOWN
PENN QUARTER

●●● *to Metro Center*

●● *to Federal Triangle, or McPherson Square*

●● *to Archives-Navy Memorial, or Mt. Vernon
Square/7th Street-Convention Center*

● *to Farragut North*

●●● *to Gallery Place-Chinatown*

● SNAPSHOT ●

Washington's Downtown area, the heart of the Capital
City, is a sprawling central business district that includes
a number of museums, the well-known K Street corri-
dor where DC lawyers work and dine, and Chinatown.
Historic Penn Quarter, the revitalized part of the
Downtown area, is a mix of federal and commercial
buildings, notably the National Archives; a flourishing
theater district; museums and galleries, including the
National Portrait Gallery and the Smithsonian
American Museum of Art, the International Spy
Museum, and Newseum; and a number of excellent
places to eat. As you walk southeast on Pennsylvania
Avenue, you'll note the great view of the U.S. Capitol in

the distance. You'll also see federal workers hurrying to work, and tourists studying their maps. It's all part of the energy of Downtown.

There is a lot to see and do here but be prepared to walk, or plan to take the Metro or a bus. For example, ride the Metro's Yellow, Red, or Green Lines to Gallery Place-Chinatown to see the world's largest Chinese Arch, the Friendship Arch, fashioned from 7,000 pieces of glazed tile *(7th St. and H, NW)*. From here you can explore Chinatown and reach the Verizon Center and surrounding eateries.

PLACES TO SEE
Landmarks:
One of the most impressive federal buildings—for its sheer size, soaring rotunda, and arched skylight—is the **Ronald Reagan Building and International Trade Center (1)** *(1300 Pennsylvania Ave. NW, 202-312-1300, www. itcdc.com)*. Filling two city blocks, it is home to a variety of government offices, the venue of **The Capitol Steps (17)**, a musical political satire troupe *(see page 119)*, cafés, a food court, and free live entertainment in summer.

The **DC Visitor Information Center** *(www.dcchamber.org, 202-289-8317, M–F 8:30AM–5:30PM)* is located here, too. Continue southeast on Pennsylvania Avenue to **The Old Post Office Pavilion (2)** *(1100 Pennsylvania Ave. NW, 202-289-4224, www.oldpost officedc.com, Mar–Aug M–Sa 10AM–8PM, Su noon–7PM; Sep–Feb M–Sa*

10AM–7PM, Su noon–6PM), an 1899 Romanesque-style U.S. Post Office. It's now a popular shopping and dining destination. Take the free elevator *(Memorial Day–Labor Day, 9AM–8PM, Su 10AM–6PM, Labor Day–Memorial Day M–Sa 9AM–5PM, Su 10AM–6PM)* to check out the amazing view from the observation deck of the 315-foot clock tower.

See the Declaration of Independence, Constitution, Bill of Rights, Emancipation Proclamation, and the Louisiana Purchase up close at the **National Archives Building (3)** *(700 Pennsylvania Ave. NW, 202-357-5000, www.archives.gov, Mar 15–Labor Day M–Sa 10AM–7PM; day after Labor Day–Mar 14 10AM–5:30PM)*. The National Archives Experience is impressive; you should plan to spend at least 90 minutes at this visitor-friendly facility. First, you'll view an 11-minute introductory

 film in the 290-seat William G. McGowan Theater. Then you're invited to tour the Archives' three exhibit galleries. The Lawrence F. O'Brien changing exhibit showcases specific collections of holdings, such as eyewitness accounts of key moments in American history. The Public Vaults permanent exhibit offers an insider glimpse into the stacks and vaults of the National Archives. Here you can access more than 1,000 fascinating records, including Oval Office audio recordings and Abraham Lincoln's telegrams to his generals. Interactive exhibits also allow visitors to "touch" and explore some

of the most interesting documents, photographs, and films in the Archives' holdings. The Rotunda for the Charters of Freedom is the home of the Declaration of Independence, Constitution, and Bill of Rights.

Note: Without reservations it may take an hour or more to enter the Archives through the general public entry, especially in the spring, over Thanksgiving weekend, and the week between Christmas and New Year's Day. You should be prepared to wait outdoors. Best, though, to skip the line altogether and make reservations in advance at www.recreation.gov. Your visit date and time will be scheduled and a confirmation will be sent; you must present it upon entry.

Next door to the Archives, the **Federal Trade Commission (4)** *(600 Pennsylvania Ave. NW, www.ftc.gov)* focuses on consumer protection and anti-competitive business practices. Check out the appropriately allegorical and nearly identical "Man Restraining Trade" statues out front. Further east, for programs related to Canadian culture, visit the strikingly designed **Canadian Embassy (5)** *(501 Pennsylvania Ave. NW, 202-682-1740,*

www.canadianembassy.org, M–F 9AM–5PM). One of the most compelling outdoor memorials is that of the nearby **U.S. Navy Memorial and Navy Heritage Center (6)** *(701 Pennsylvania Ave. NW, 202-737-2300, www.navymemorial.org, daily 9:30AM–5PM).* Memorial Plaza features a 100-foot granite map of the world and a seven-foot statue of the Lone Sailor. Bronze for the statue was mixed with artifacts from U.S. Navy ships, including the U.S.S. *Constitution* ("Old Ironsides"). Official ceremonies and

outdoor concerts draw locals and visitors. The adjacent Naval Heritage Center houses rotating exhibits about service at sea. The **J. Edgar Hoover Building (7)** *(935 Pennsylvania Ave. NW)* is home to the Federal Bureau of Investigation. While the FBI used to offer a popular tour of its headquarters, tours have been suspended.

Follow H Street east to the **Martin Luther King, Jr. Memorial Library (8)** *(901 G St. NW, 202-727-0321, www.dclibrary.org/mlk, M–Tu noon–9PM, W–Sa 9:30AM–5:30PM, Su 1PM–5PM)*, the District's central library branch and the only DC building designed by modern master Ludwig Mies van der Rohe. A mural by Don Miller depicts Dr. King's life and the history of the Civil Rights movement. **Newseum (9)** *(555 Pennsylvania Ave. NW, 888-639-7386, www.newseum.org, daily 9AM–5PM)* is totally interactive—there is a breaking news feed and visitors can create their own newscasts. Exhibits span five centuries of news from all media. Highlights include a gallery of Pulitzer Prize-winning photos and "What's News," a video montage of the most important news clips of all time. Bring your camera and strike a pose with the life-like wax figures of a myriad of VIPs, from George Washington to George Clooney, at **Madame Tussauds (10)** *(1001 F St. NW, 866-823-9565,* *www.madametussauds.com, open 365 days a year at 10AM, call for updated hours).*

Arts & Entertainment:

Washington's thriving theater district offers both
avant-garde productions
and national touring shows.
The **National Theatre (11)**
*(1321 Pennsylvania Ave. NW, 202-628-6161,
www.nationaltheatre.org, box office M–Sa 10AM–6PM, Su
noon–6PM or until showtime on performance nights)* features tours of Broadway shows, pre-Broadway shows, and
American premieres. The **Warner Theatre (12)** *(513 13th
St. NW, 202-783-4000, www.warnertheatre.com)* hosts
Broadway productions, comedies, dance performances,
films, and concerts. You'll love its marble and gilded lobby
and chandelier-lit auditorium. There is a "Walk of Fame"
on the sidewalk in front with stars of the artists who have
performed here, including Frank Sinatra, Bonnie Raitt,
and Chris Rock. **Ford's Theatre (13)** *(511 10th St. NW,
202-347-4833, www.fordstheatre.org, tour hours daily
9AM–5PM; box office hours daily 8:30AM–6PM or until 8PM on
performance nights)* is the place where actor John Wilkes
Booth shot Abraham Lincoln on April 14, 1865; today,
it still operates as a working theater. Admission to the
Ford Theatre National Historic Site requires a free timed
entry ticket available at the box office or for a small fee at
www.ticketmaster.com. One-hour tour includes either a
National Park Ranger presentation on the theater's history or a short one-act Civil War-themed play. Ticket allows

admission to the Ford Theatre Museum on the lower level (where you can see the pistol used by Booth and the clothing Lincoln wore that night), as well as the newly renovated the Peterson House across the street, where Lincoln died. The renowned **Shakespeare Theatre Company/Harman Center for the Arts** *(www.shakespeare theatre.org, 202-547-1122)* has been called "the nation's foremost Shakespeare company" by the *Wall Street Journal* and has not one, but two, venues in the neighborhood. **Lansburgh Theatre (14)** *(450 7th St. NW, box office M–Sa 10AM–6PM, Su noon–6PM or until showtime on performance nights)* and the brand-new state-of-the-art **Sidney Harman Hall (15)** *(6th and F Sts. NW, box office M–Sa 10AM–6PM, Su noon–6PM or until showtime on performance nights)*. Harman is also the location for the company's very popular "Summer Shakespeare Free For All" performances. The **Woolly Mammoth Theatre Company (16)** *(641 D St. NW, 202-393-3939, www.woollymammoth.net, box office hours M–F 10AM–6PM, open Sa–Su noon–6PM performance weeks only)* performs and premieres experimental plays by emerging writers. Featuring musical political satire, **The Capitol Steps (17)** *(Ronald Reagan Building, 13th and Pennsylvania Ave. NW, 202-312-1555, www.capsteps.com, F–Sa 7:30PM)*, made up of Capitol Hill staffers and other performers, are famous for hilarious musical political satire.

Investigate the **International Spy Museum (18)** *(800 F St. NW, 202-393-7798, www.spymuseum.org, May–Labor Day 9AM–7PM; day after Labor Day–Nov 10AM–6PM, Dec–Apr,* *check Web site for times)*, a must-see for families with teens. The museum is home to the world's largest collection of international espionage artifacts, from concealment devices, sabotage weapons, and cipher machines to dead drops, secret writings, and microdots.

The **National Portrait Gallery (19)** *(8th/F Sts. NW, 202-633-8300, www.npg.si.edu, daily 11:30AM–7PM)* with its thousands of images of American citizens, strives to present "history with personality," while the **Smithsonian American Art Museum (19)** *(8th/F Sts. NW, 202-633-7970, www.americanart.si.edu, daily 11:30AM–7PM)* showcases the works of American artists at their best. Both museums are located in the former Patent Office, one of DC's oldest public buildings. This acclaimed Greek Revival structure, with its double curving staircase and two city block-long skylights, dates from 1836, when it was the home of the U.S. Patent Office.

The portrait gallery collection includes thousands of the world's most compelling paintings, sculptures, drawings, and photographs of notable Americans, from the famous "Lansdowne" portrait of George Washington and the "cracked plate" portrait of Abraham Lincoln to Shepard Fairey's "Hope" poster of Barack Obama. Don't forget to check out the 3rd floor exhibit, "20th Century Americans," which includes portraits of Babe Ruth, Rosa Parks, Marilyn Monroe, and other notables.

The Smithsonian is home to the first U.S. federal art collection. Its holdings include colonial portraiture, 19th-century landscapes, American impressionism, 20th-century realism and abstraction, New Deal projects, sculpture, photography, contemporary crafts, and African American, Latino, and folk art. More than 7,000 American artists are represented, including Winslow Homer, John Singer Sargent, Childe Hassam, Georgia O'Keeffe, Edward Hopper, Andrew Wyeth, Nam June Paik, and Martin Puryear. You'll also want to stop by the museum's **Lunder Conservation Center**; this unique facility allows you to observe conservators caring for the museums' national treasures through floor-to-ceiling windows. The **Luce Foundation for American Art** occupies three floors of the museum's west wing and affords visitors access to an additional 3,300 densely displayed museum pieces.

Art begets art. In this neighborhood, you'll also find a cluster of art galleries spotlighting local and national artists. **Gallery at Flashpoint (20)** *(916 G St. NW, 202-315-1310, www.flashpointdc.org, Tu–Sa noon–6PM)* houses both an art gallery and performance art space. **Civilian Art Projects (21)** *(1019 7th St. NW, 202-607-3804, www.civilianart projects.com, W, Th, Sa 1PM–6PM)* represents emerging artists.

Touchstone Gallery (22) *(901 New York Ave. NW, 202-347-2787, www.touchstonegallery.com, W–Th 11AM–6PM, F 11AM–8PM)* is an artist cooperative featuring affordable contemporary art. The **Edison Place Gallery (23)** *(702 8th St. NW, 202-872-3396, www.pepco.com, Tu–F noon–4PM)*, on the ground floor of Pepco headquarters, often features the work of nonprofits.

The **National Museum of Crime & Punishment (24)** *(575 7th St. NW, 202-393-1099, www.crimemuseum.org, May 21–Aug 31: M–Th 9AM–7PM, F–Sa 9AM–8PM, Su 10AM–7PM; Sept 1–May 20: Su–Th 10AM–7PM, F–Sa 10AM–8pm; tickets are date and time sensitive, call 202-621-5550 to purchase by phone)* offers over 100 exhibits, including an interactive CSI experience. The **National Geographic Museum at Explorers Hall (25)** *(1145 17th St. NW, 202-857-7588, www.nationalgeographic.com/museum, daily 9AM–5PM)* presents a variety of changing exhibits. **National Museum of Women in the Arts (26)** *(1250 New York Ave. NW, 202-783-5000 or 800-222-7270, www.nmwa.org, M–Sa 10AM–5PM, Su noon–5PM)* showcases more than 3,000 works by women, including Mary Cassatt, Frida Kahlo, and Louise Nevelson. The **Sixth and I Synagogue (27)** *(600 I St. NW, 202-408-3100, www.sixthandi.org)* is a unique non-denominational cultural center. Check out its events calendar and look for its kosher "Sixth & Rye" food truck around town. The **Goethe-Institut (28)** *(812 7th St. NW, 202-289-1200, www.goethe.de/washington,*

M–Th 9AM–5PM, F 9AM–3PM), a German cultural center, shows films, presents art exhibits, and runs discussions and language classes. The **Lillian & Albert Small Jewish Museum (29)** *(corner of 3rd and G Sts. NW, www.jhsgw.org, M, Tu, Th 1PM–4PM)* is dedicated to the story of the local Jewish community. The **Verizon Center (30)** *(601 F St. NW, 202-628-3200, www.verizon-center.com, box office hours 10:30AM–5:30PM, additional box office at 7th and G St. open during event hours)*, is home to NBA's Washington Wizards, NHL's Washington Capitals, WNBA's Washington Mystics, and the Georgetown Hoyas men's basketball team. Interested in architecture? Don't miss the **National Building Museum (31)** *(401 F St. NW, 202-272-2448, www.nbm.org, M–Sa 10AM–5PM, Su 11AM–5PM)*.

Enjoy its Great Hall, museum shop, café, or docent-led tours of its stunning landmark building for free; admission prices offer access to LEGO® Architecture, kids' Building Zone, and other galleries and tours. Learn about the latest scientific research at the **Marian Koshland Science Museum (32)** *(6th and E Sts. NW, 202-334-1201, www.koshland-science-museum.org, W–M 10AM–6PM)*, operated by the National Academy of Sciences. Recommended for kids over age 10.

☆ ☆ ☆ ☆

PLACES TO EAT & DRINK
Where to Eat:

For lively dining with plenty of variety, the Downtown area fills the bill. **Againn DC (33) ($$)** *(1099 New York Ave. NW, 202-639-9830, www.againndc.com, M–Th 11:30AM–11PM, F 11:30AM–midnight, Sa 5:30PM–midnight)* offers satisfying pub food; try the heritage pork belly with cracklings. The **Capital Grille (34) ($$$)** *(601 Pennsylvania Ave. NW, 202-737-6200, www.thecapitalgrille.com, M–Th 11:30AM–3PM, 5PM–10PM, F–Sa 11:30AM–3PM, 5PM–11PM, Su 5PM–10PM)* is known for its dry aged steaks, seafood, chops, and service. Star chef José Andrés juggles several ventures in DC, including **Café Atlantico (35) ($$)** *(405 8th St. NW, 202-393-0812, www.cafeatlantico.com, Su, Tu, Th 11:30AM–2:30PM,*

5PM–10PM, F–Sa 11:30AM–2:30PM, 5PM–11PM), a favorite for its innovative Nuevo Latin-style food. A hotspot for years, **Rasika (36) ($$)** *(633 D St. NW, 202-637-1222, www.rasikarestaurant.com, M–Th 11:30AM–2:30PM, 5:30PM–10:30PM, F 11:30AM–2:30PM, 5:30PM–11PM, Sa 5PM–11PM)*—the name is derived from a Sanskrit word for "flavors"—is still going strong. Everyone gets the palak chaat, the crispy spinach appetizer with sweet yogurt, tamarind, and date chutney. **Hard Rock Café (37) ($$)** *(999 E. St. NW, 202-737-7625, www.hardrockcafe.com, Su–Th 11AM–11PM, F–Sa 11AM–*

midnight) has a DC location too. **TenPenh (38) ($$)** *(1001 Pennsylvania Ave. NW, 202-393-4500, www.tenpenh.com, M–Th 11:30AM–2:30PM, 5:30PM–10:30PM, F 11:30AM–2:30PM, 5:30PM–11PM, Sa 5:30PM–11PM, Su 5:30PM–9:30PM)* presents tasty Southeast Asian dishes, from red Thai curry shrimp, to peanut-crusted tuna, to Asian pear bread pudding. For a quick pick-me-up, consider **Teaism (39) ($)** *(400 8th St. NW, 202-638-6010, www.*

teaism.com, M–F 7:30AM–10PM, Sa–Su 9:30AM–9PM), serving specialty teas, cookies, and Pan-Asian meals, including bento boxes with teriyaki salmon, meatballs, or grilled veggies. Go Belgian at **Brasserie Beck (40) $$-$$$** *(1101 K St. NW, 202-408-1717, www.beckdc.com, lunch M–F 11:30AM–5PM, dinner M–Th 5PM–11PM, F–Sa 5PM–11PM, Su 4PM–9PM, brunch/lunch Sa–Su 11:30AM–4PM)* with mussels, oysters, frites, and an extensive list of beers from Belgium. Its stunning space evokes a European railway station. José Andrés also brings sophisticated Mexican cuisine to DC with **Oyamel (41) ($)** *(401 7th St. NW, 202-628-1005, www.oyamel.com, Su–M 11:30AM–10PM, Tu–Th 11:30AM–11:30PM, F–Sa 11:30AM–*

midnight). The margaritas are *fuerte*, the red snapper Vera Cruz a stand out, and the mole-fried potatoes with a touch of chocolate, fantastic. (Dare you to order the grasshopper tacos!) Sip a "spy-tini" as you snoop on neighboring diners (or the chef) through strategically placed portholes at **Zola (42) ($$–$$$)** *(800 F St. NW, 202-654-0999, www.zoladc.com, M–Th 11:30AM–10PM, F–Sa 11:30AM–11PM, Su 11:30AM–9PM)*, named for French novelist Émile Zola. Red velvet booths and art made from declassified CIA documents add to the ambience; the menu includes inventive New American dishes. For a quick meal, **Spy City Café (43) ($)** *(800 F St. NW, 202-654-0995, www.spymuseum.org, M–F 8AM–6PM, Sa–Su 10AM–5PM)* next door offers soups, sandwiches, and pizza. Buzzing **Zaytinya (44) ($$–$$$)** *(701 9th St. NW, 202-638-0800, www.zaytinya.com, Su–M 11:30AM–10PM, Tu 11:30AM–11:30PM, F–Sa 11:30AM–midnight)* is José Andrés's ode to the cuisines of Greece, Turkey, and

Lebanon, and offers a modern take on traditional mezze (appetizers). Try the grilled octopus in yellow split peas, or goat cheese wrapped in grape leaves. For dessert: Turkish coffee chocolate cake. **Austin Grill (45) ($)** *(750 E. St. NW, 202-393-3776, www.austingrill.com, M–Th 11AM–11PM, F–Sa 11AM–midnight, Su 11AM–10PM)* rustles up reliable, reasonable Tex-Mex food in a lively atmosphere. Within the **Ronald Reagan Building and International Trade Center (1)**, **Aria Pizzeria & Bar (46) ($)** *(1300 Pennsylvania Ave. NW, 202-312-1250, www.ariapizzeria.com, M–Tu 11:30AM–5PM, W–Th 11:30AM–9PM, F 11:30AM–10PM, Sa 5PM–10PM)* offers hearth-baked pizza, panini, and pastas. Enjoy live music on the outdoor patio during warm weather. For Latin American that dazzles, dine at **Ceiba (47) ($$-$$$)** *(701 14th St. at G St. NW, 202-393-3983, www.ceiba restaurant.com, M–Th 11:30AM–2:30PM, 5:30PM–10:30PM, F 11:30AM–2:30PM, 5:30PM–11PM, Sa 5:30PM–11PM, Su 5PM–9PM).* Pronounced "say-ba," it

features dishes from Yucatanian, Brazilian, Peruvian, and Cuban traditions. **DC Coast Restaurant (48) ($$-$$$)** *(1401 K St. NW, 202-216-5988, www.dccoast.com, M–Th 11:30AM–2:30PM, 5:30PM–10:30PM, F 11:30AM–2:30PM, 5:30PM–11PM, Sa 5:30PM–11PM, Su 5:30PM–9PM),* with a lively Art Deco bar, serves American cuisine with a Gulf Coast influence. Try its seafood gumbo or famous Chinese-style smoked lobster. Romantic haven **Coeur de Lion (49) ($$-$$$)** *(Henley Park Hotel, 926 Massachusetts Ave. NW, 202-414-0500, www.henleypark. com, M–Sa 7AM–10:30AM, 11:30AM–2:30PM, 6PM–11PM, Su 11:30AM–2:30PM, 6PM–11PM)* offers elegant dining under crystal chandeliers. The menu combines fresh seafood, seasonal ingredients, and market finds. Daily afternoon tea is a lovely respite from sightseeing. The popular **District Chop House (50) ($$-$$$)** *(509 7th St. at E St. NW, 202-347-3434, www.chophouse.com, M–Th 11AM–11PM, F–Sa 11AM–11:30PM, Su 11AM–10PM)* is located less than a block from the Verizon Center. Sample a beer from its on-site brewery. Enjoy a steak or brick-oven pizza. A full-service Scotch and bourbon bar, billiard tables, and cigar lounge will

round out your experience here. The **Morrison-Clark (51) ($$-$$$)** *(Massachusetts Ave. and 11th St. NW, 202-898-1200, www. morrisonclark.com, M–Sa 7AM–10AM, 11AM–2PM, 6PM–10PM, Su 11AM–2PM, 6PM–9PM)*, with marble fireplaces, gilded mirrors, and lace curtains, is a gem. Dine alfresco in its charming courtyard. The American/Continental menu is imbued with Southern flavor. Bourbon shrimp with grits is a popular choice. For Louisiana-style cuisine, **Acadiana (52) ($$)** *(901 New York Ave. NW, 202-408-8848, www.acadianarestaurant.com, M–Th 11:30AM–2:30PM, 5:30PM–10:30PM, F 11:30AM–2:30PM, 5:30PM–11PM, Sa 5:30PM–11PM, Su 11AM–2:30PM, 5:30PM–9:30PM)* is the place. Its New Orleans–style barbecue shrimp was named a *USA Today* "Top 25 Dish." In summer, stop by for "Big Easy" Happy Hour on the patio. The **Oceanaire Seafood Room (53) ($$$)** *(1201 F St. NW, 202-347-BASS, www.oceanaire.com, M–Th 11:30AM–10PM, F 11:30AM–11PM, Sa 5PM–11PM, Su 5PM–9PM)*, reminiscent of a swanky 1930s ocean liner, serves some of the freshest seafood in town, flown in daily. For Tuscan-style Italian prepared in an open-air kitchen, try **Tuscana West**  **(54) ($$)** *(1350 I St. NW, 202-289-7300, www. tuscanawest.net, M–F 11:30AM–10PM, Sa 5PM–10PM)*. **Café Promenade (55) ($$-$$$)** *(Renaissance Mayflower*

Hotel, 1127 Connecticut Ave. NW, 202-347-2233, daily 6:30AM–10:30PM) serves up great American breakfasts, working lunches, and dinner fare. Chinatown offers a number of Cantonese, Szechuan, Hunan, and Mongolian eateries. **Full Kee (56) ($)** *(509 H St. NW, 202-371-2233, www.fullkeedc.com, daily 11AM–2AM)* is a local favorite for its satisfying menu and affordable prices. Try any of the soups with roast meat, steamed dumplings, or eggplant with garlic sauce.

Bars & Nightlife:

Whether you are a beer dabbler or a brew snob, **RFD Washington (57)** *(810 7th St. NW, 202-289-2030, www.lovethebeer.com, M–Th 11AM–2AM, F–Sa 11AM–3AM, Su noon–midnight)* has a beer for you. RFD (Regional Food and Drink) boasts more than 300 different bottled beers and has an extensive tap selection. Cool **Rocket Bar (58)** *(714 7th St. NW, 202-628-7665, www.rocketbardc.com, Su–Th 4PM–2AM, F–Sa 4PM–3AM)*, with pool tables, darts, and shuffleboards, attracts a late-night crowd. **Fado (59)** *(808 7th St. NW, 202-789-0066, www.fadoirishpub.com, Su–Th 11AM–2AM, F–Sa 11AM–3AM)* is an Irish pub in the midst of Chinatown. Just about every element of its decor—from the stones in the floor to the etched wood— was imported from Ireland. Patrons enjoy its Celtic rock shows, trivia nights, and menu choices like corned beef and cabbage. Mingle with local athletes and DC politicos/celebrities at **Lucky Strike Lanes and Lounge (60)** *(701 7th St. NW, 202-347-1021, www.bowllucky strike.com, Su–Th noon–1AM, F–Sa noon–2AM)*, a snazzy bowling alley/cocktail lounge. Play pool or watch the game on TV as you wait for a lane. After 8PM, it's 21 and older only. **Lux Lounge (61)** *(649 New York Ave. NW, 202-347-8100, www.luxloungedc.com, F–Sa 9PM–3AM,*

Su 9PM–1AM) is an upscale dance club where the DJs spin hip hop, jazz, and Top 40 for a young and sexy crowd. **Co Co Sala (62)** *(929 F St. NW, 202-347-4265, www.cocosala.com, M–Th 11AM–1:30AM, F 11AM–2:30AM, Sa brunch 11AM–3PM, 5PM–2:30AM, Su 11AM–3PM)* features small plates dining options and scrumptious chocolate desserts during the day. After dark, it's a sophisticated chocolate lounge. The signature drink: the *Co Cojito*—made with chocolate-infused vodka. Late night DJ music adds to the vibe.

WHERE TO SHOP

Gallery Place (63) *(7th and H Sts. NW, www.gallery place.com, retail and dining hours vary)* is home to a 14-screen Regal Cinema, Ann Taylor Loft, Urban Outfitters, Häagen-Dazs, and Aveda, among other shops. At **Fahrney's (64)** *(1317 F St. NW, 202-628-9525, www.fahrneyspens.com, M–F 9:30AM–6PM, Sa 10AM–5PM)*, established in 1929, you can purchase fine writing

instruments, stationery, gifts, and desk accessories. Forget to pack something? You can likely replace it at **Macy's (65)** *(1201 G. St. NW, 202-628-6661, www.macys.com, M–Sa 10AM–8PM, Su noon–6PM)* department store. **Coup de Foudre Lingerie (66)** *(1008 E St. NW, 202-393-0878, www. coupdefoudrelingerie.com, M–Sa 11AM– 6PM)* stocks wispy European lingerie. Treat yourself!

WHERE TO STAY

The **Courtyard Washington Convention Center (67)** *($$- $$$)* *(900 F St. NW, 202-638-4600 or 800-321- 2211, www.courtyard.com/wascn)*, a restored historic landmark, is a comfortable place to stay across from the **International Spy Museum (18)** and a block from the **Verizon Center (30)**. **Hotel Harrington (68)** *($)* *(436 11th St. NW, 202-628-8140 or 800-424-8532, www.hotel-harrington.com)* is a friendly, family-owned hotel convenient to museums, theaters, and the Old Post Office Pavilion. It offers 26 deluxe family rooms, some of which will accommodate six people. For luxury with a twist, book the vibrant **Hotel Monaco (69)** *($$$)* *(700 F St. NW, 202-628- 7177, www.monaco-dc.com)*; your stay includes "Guppy Love," a companion goldfish to keep you company. (Housekeeping cares for your finned friend.) The **Renaissance Mayflower Hotel (70)** *($$$)* *(1127 Connecticut*

Ave. NW, 202-347-3000 or 800-228-7697, www.renaissancehotels.com) is one of the largest, most historic, and loveliest hotels in Washington. Calvin Coolidge's inaugural ball took place here. Want to be in the heart of the city, close to the Convention Center? Stay at the **Grand Hyatt Washington (71)** (**$$-$$$**) *(1000 H St. NW, 202-582-1234 or 800-223-1234, www.grandwashington.hyatt.com)*; it features a soaring atrium, an indoor "lagoon" with a 35-foot waterfall, six restaurants and bars, and access to the Metro Center. **Henley Park Hotel (72)** (**$$-$$$**) *(926 Massachusetts Ave. NW, 202-638-5200 or 800-222-8474, www.henleypark.com)* is a restored Tudor-style hotel with gargoyles, leaded windows, Edwardian furnishings, and "white glove" service. It's located one block from the Convention Center. Tea is served daily at 4PM. The **Morrison-Clark Inn (73)** (**$$-$$$**) *(Massachusetts Ave. and 11th St. NW, 202-898-1200 or 800-222-8474, www.morrisonclark.com)* is comprised of two Victorian town houses.

Evoking the spirit and aesthetic sensibility of our third president, The Jefferson (74) ($$$) *(1200 16th St. NW, 202-347-2200 or 800-332-7898, www.jeffersondc.com)* even showcases original documents signed by Jefferson. This boutique hotel has a residential feel, a reputation for exceptional service, and is located just four blocks from the White House.

chapter 5

UPPER NORTHWEST
AND ENVIRONS

ADAMS MORGAN

UPPER NORTHWEST AND ENVIRONS

ADAMS MORGAN

Places to See:

1. Fort Reno Park
2. Rock Creek Park
3. Klingle Mansion
4. Kennedy-Warren Apartment Building
5. WASHINGTON NATIONAL CATHEDRAL ★
6. Islamic Center
7. NATIONAL ZOOLOGICAL PARK ★
8. Rock Creek Park Nature Center and Planetarium
9. Rock Creek Park Horse Center
10. Uptown Theater
11. Avalon Theatre
12. Hillwood Museum & Gardens
37. Three Macaws Mural
38. Meridian International Center
39. Cows on a Bicycle Mural
40. Mexican Cultural Institute
41. Toulouse-Lautrec Mural
42. Madam's Organ Mural
43. District of Columbia Arts Center
44. Champorama Park Mural
45. Meridian Hill Park

Places to Eat & Drink:

13. Sushiko
14. New Heights
15. Lebanese Taverna
16. Ardeo
17. Firehook Bakery and Coffee House
18. Indique
19. Booeymonger
20. 2 Amys Pizza
21. Café Olé
22. Breadsoda
23. Café Deluxe
24. Bourbon Glover Park
46. Mama Ayesha's Restaurant
47. Meskerem
48. The Grill from Ipanema
49. Cashion's Eat Place
50. Mixtec
51. Perry's
52. Pasta Mia
53. Soussi
54. Habana Village

★ *Top Pick*

Washington is a city of
Southern efficiency and
Northern charm.

—John F. Kennedy

UPPER NORTHWEST AND ENVIRONS

● *to Woodley Park-Zoo/Adams Morgan,
or Cleveland Park, or Van Ness-UDC,
or Tenleytown-AU, or Friendship Heights*

● SNAPSHOT ●

Upper Northwest—located northwest of the nearly 1,800 acres of Rock Creek Park—offers several interesting places to see, including the National Zoo, Washington National Cathedral, and the Hillwood Museum and Gardens, while popular restaurants dot Connecticut and Wisconsin Avenues. The U.S. Naval Observatory and the campus of American University are also in this area. Rock Creek Park dates back to 1866, when a senate committee sought to locate an attractive tract of land for the presidential mansion. Though the chief executive's home was never situated here, the park became a place of respite and relaxation for locals and visitors. Park-goers enjoy cycling, golfing, picnicking, horseback riding, or wandering through the area's natural beauty. Rock Creek Parkway wends its way through the park, offering motorists lovely scenic views. Most places of interest in Upper Northwest are accessible by Metro. Some call

Connecticut Avenue a "corridor," and it is an appropriate description, as nearby attractions are like "rooms" situated off it.

PLACES TO SEE
Landmarks:

Fort Reno Park (1) *(Chesapeake St. and Nebraska Ave. NW)* is the highest point in DC, and was once used as

a Civil War fort. Its free summer rock concerts are a Washington tradition. The most striking feature of Upper Northwest, however, is **Rock Creek Park (2)** *(Beach Drive NW, open daily dawn–dusk)*, a tranquil oasis in the capital city. The park also contains Civil War–era ruins, a nature center and planetarium, and the **Carter Barron Amphitheatre**. Wildlife abounds—don't be surprised if you catch a glimpse of deer, coyotes, foxes, or beavers. There are numerous entrances to Rock Creek, including the one at the **Klingle Mansion (3)** *(3545 Williamsburg Ln. NW, 202-895-6070, www.nps.gov/rocr, W–Su 9AM–5PM)*, a large stone farm-

house built in 1823 that serves as the park's headquarters. Outside Rock Creek, in the Cleveland Park Historic District, you'll find a number of landmarks near the Cleveland Park Metro stop, including historic mansions that were once summer retreats.

The **Kennedy-Warren Apartment Building (4)** *(3133 Connecticut Ave. NW)* is a renowned Aztec/Art Deco masterpiece that has been home to a variety of distinguished residents, among them Lyndon B. and "Lady Bird" Johnson, author P. J. O'Rourke, and, during World War II, numerous generals and admirals.

The ★**WASHINGTON NATIONAL CATHEDRAL (5)** *(Massachusetts and Wisconsin Aves. NW, 202-537-6200, www.nationalcathedral.org; 30 minute guided tours; M–F 10AM–11:30AM, 1PM–4PM, Sa 10AM–11:30AM, 1PM–3:30PM, Su 1PM–2:30PM)*, officially known as the Cathedral Church of St. Peter and St. Paul, has served as the site for major services, such as Ronald Reagan's state funeral. Martin Luther King, Jr. preached his last Sunday sermon from its pulpit on March 31, 1968; he was assassinated four days later. Helen Keller and her tutor Annie Sullivan are buried here, as is Woodrow Wilson. Though affiliated with the Episcopal Church, its doors are open to all faiths. Nearly the length of two football fields, the massive limestone structure is the second largest cathedral in the U.S. and sixth largest in the world. Its central, 300-foot Gloria in Excelsis Tower is the highest point in the District of Columbia. Seventy windows in the seventh-floor Pilgrim Observation Gallery provide panoramic views. Designed by leading British Gothic architect George Frederick Bodley after medieval cathedrals, this 20th-century architectural marvel features flying buttresses, 215 stained-glass windows, 110 gargoyles, and a 53-bell carillon.

TOP PICK!

The cathedral's cornerstone, which came from the Bethlehem region, was inset into a larger piece of American granite. It was laid by Theodore Roosevelt and the Bishop of London in 1907; construction was completed in 1990. The cathedral's high altar is made from stones quarried near Jerusalem. The pulpit is constructed from stones from Canterbury Cathedral, and the stone for the bishop's formal seat, or *cathedra* (the origin of the word "cathedral"), comes from ancient Glastonbury Abbey. You'll find the cathedral filled with American commemoratives, such as statues of Washington and Lincoln, state flags, floor-inlaid state seals, and stained-glass windows depicting special achievements, such as the Lewis and Clark expedition. The Space Window honors man's landing on the moon, and even includes a fragment of lunar rock! Don't miss the gargoyles and grotesques, including a boar, a braying donkey, a cat, a dog, and Darth Vader. For a colorful and fragrance-filled interlude, stop at the cathedral's Herb Cottage or stroll the medieval Bishop's Garden. Handouts are provided for self-guided tours. Or take advantage of the cathedral's variety of specialized tours, from gargoyle tours and tea tours to garden tours and woodland walks, spotlighting the cathedral's 57 acres of grounds on Mount Saint Alban. Tour fee donations support the cathedral's programs and ministry. The cathedral is 1-1/2 miles from the Tenleytown–AU Metro stop on the Red Line. Or take the #30, #32, #34, or #36 bus south.

Arts & Entertainment:

The **Islamic Center (6)** *(2551 Massachusetts Ave. NW, 202-332-8343, www.theislamiccenter.com)* is located in a white limestone building topped with a 160-foot minaret. It's filled with art from the Middle East, including Persian carpets and stained-glass windows. It also contains a library and hosts lectures.

The ★**NATIONAL ZOOLOGICAL PARK (7)** *(3001 Connecticut Ave. NW, 202-633-4800, www.natzoo.si.edu, Apr–Oct 10AM–6PM, Nov–Mar 10AM–4:30PM)*, or more simply, the

TOP PICK!

National Zoo, is part of the Smithsonian Institution and is an ideal attraction for the entire family. **Tip:** The entrance to the zoo is midway between two Metro stations. If you arrive at Woodley Park-Zoo, you need to walk uphill. Try arriving at Cleveland Park so you can walk downhill to the Connecticut Avenue entrance. Set in 163 acres within Rock Creek National Park, the zoo is home for about 2,000 animals from 400 different species. The pandas, of course, are among the most popular. They are on loan from China until at least 2015. Mei

Xiang and Tian Tian have produced one boy panda cub, Tai Shan, who was born in 2005 and returned to the China Conservation and Research Center in 2010. He is missed!

The National Zoo has lions, tigers, bears, Komodo dragons, red wolves, and much more, including the exhibit Amazonia, a re-created tropical rain forest. An

"O-Line" system of cables and towers between the Think Tank and the Ape House allows the orangutans to swing about 35 feet over your head between buildings. For early risers, the Zoo's grounds open at 6AM. Morning is a great time to visit the animals exhibited outdoors—they are more active and the crowds are smaller. **Rock Creek Park Nature Center and Planetarium (8)** *(Rock Creek Park, 5200 Glover Rd. NW, 202-895-6070, W–Su 9AM–5PM)* is another great place for kids. There are guided walks on weekends, a hands-on Discovery Room, and a planetarium. The **Rock Creek Park Horse Center (9)** *(5100 Glover Rd. NW, 202-362-0117, www.rockcreekhorsecenter.com, Tu–F noon–6PM, Sa–Su 9AM–5PM)* next door offers guided trail rides. Like outdoor entertainment? **Carter Barron Amphitheatre** in upper Rock Creek *(4850 Colorado Ave. NW, 202-426-0486, www.nps.gov/rocr, box office noon–8PM on performance days)* hosts Shakespeare and other productions and concerts all summer long in a 4,200-seat venue with outstanding natural acoustics. The largest movie screen in DC can be found at the Art Deco **Uptown Theater (10)** *(3426 Connecticut Ave. NW, 202-966-8805, www.amctheatres.com/Uptown1/)*. Opened

in 1933, the Uptown is a treasure; a renovated classic theater with a single screen. The landmark **Avalon Theatre (11)** *(5612 Connecticut Ave. NW, just south of Chevy Chase Cir., 202-966-6000, www.theavalon.org)* has been a popular gathering place for families since 1923, especially after air-conditioning was installed in 1937. It now shows foreign, independent, and documentary films. Closer to the Van Ness–UDC Metro stop, you'll spot the stately **Hillwood** **Museum & Gardens (12)** *(4155 Linnean Ave. NW, Upton/Tilden Sts., 202-686-5807; www.hillwood museum.org, Tu–Sa 10AM–5PM, closed Jan)*. The restored estate of Marjorie Merriweather Post, heiress to the Post cereal fortune, Hillwood comprises 25 landscaped acres and a 40-room mansion filled with treasures she collected throughout the world, including Fabergé pieces and 18th- and 19th-century French furnishings. Outside, you can stroll through Mrs. Post's Japanese-style garden, rose garden, and formal French Parterre Garden. Enjoy salads, sandwiches, and other light fare at the Hillwood Café. Walking further north, you'll pass the **Walter Reed Army Medical Center** (which was closed in 2011).

PLACES TO EAT & DRINK
Where to Eat:

At **Sushiko (13) ($$)** *(2309 Wisconsin Ave., NW, www. sushikorestaurants.com, M 6PM–10:30PM, Tu–Th noon–2:30PM, 6PM–10:30PM, F noon–2:30PM, 6PM–11PM, Sa 5:30PM–11PM)* the sushi is sublime and traditional Japanese cooked specialties top notch. Standout eateries in Woodley Park include **New Heights (14) ($$$)** *(2317 Calvert St. NW, 202-234-4110, www.newheights restaurant.com, M–Th 5:30PM–10PM, F–Sa 5:30PM–10:30PM)*, offering New American cuisine. Try the pan-roasted rockfish with tamarind or rabbit loin with salted apples and speck. Popular **Lebanese Taverna (15) ($$)** *(2641 Connecticut Ave. NW, 202-265-8681, www.lebanesetaverna.com, M 11:30AM–2:30PM, 5PM–9PM, Tu–Th 11:30AM–2:30PM, 5PM–10PM, F 11:30AM–2:30PM, 5PM–11PM, Sa noon–3PM, 5PM–11PM, Su noon–9PM)* is tops in the family category with a tempting, value-priced menu and fresh bread baked on premises in a wood-burning oven. Near the Cleveland Park Metro stop, dine with politicos and media at acclaimed **Ardeo (16) ($$$)** *(3311 Connecticut Ave. NW, 202-244-6750, www.ardeo restaurant.com, Su–Th 5:30PM–10:30PM, F–Sa 5:30PM–11:30PM, Su 11AM–3PM)*, a neighborhood restaurant known for its modern American menu, incorporating Asian and Mediterranean influences in a sleek, art-filled setting. Not for nothing does the line spill out the door at **Firehook Bakery and Coffee House (17) ($)** *(3411 Connecticut Ave. NW, 202-362-2253, www.firehook.com, M–F 6:30AM–8PM, Sa–Su 7AM–8PM)*, popular for sandwiches (on exceptional bread)

and for soups, salads, and baked goods. Make dessert a Presidential Sweet—an oatmeal cookie with chocolate

chips, dried cherries, and coconut. **Indique (18) ($-$$)** *(3512–14 Connecticut Ave. NW, 202-244-6600, www.indique.com, Su–Th 5:30PM–10:30PM, F–Sa noon–3PM, 5:30PM–11PM)* prepares Indian food with new twists on dishes like Cornish game hen, served in a paste of curry leaves and hot peppers. Crowd-pleasing **Booeymonger (19) ($)** *(5252 Wisconsin Ave. NW, 202-686-5805, www.booeymonger.com, Su–Th 7:30AM–midnight, F–Sa 7:30AM–1AM)*, near the Friendship Heights Metro stop, has been turning out specialty sandwiches and wraps for more than 30 years. Kids' menu also available. DC pizza aficionados hail **2 Amys Pizza (20) ($)** *(3715 Macomb St. NW, 202-885-5700, www.2amyspizza.com, M 5PM–10PM, Tu–Th 11AM–10PM, F–Sa 11AM–11PM)* as among the best in town. This is D.O.C. *(Denominazione di Origine Controllata)* pizza, as certified by the Italian government—made in a wood-burning oven with the finest ingredients.

If you're driving, check out the restaurants clustered along Wisconsin Avenue a block or two from the **Washington National Cathedral (5)**. For small-plate Mediterranean accompanied by a microbrew, glass of wine, or a martini in a fun, friendly setting, choose **Café Olé (21) ($)** *(4000 Wisconsin Ave. NW, 202-244-1330, www.cafeoledc.com, Su–Th 11AM–9PM, F–Sa 11AM–10PM)*.

Bars & Nightlife

Unpretentious **Breadsoda (22)** *(2233 Wisconsin Ave. NW, 202-333-7445, www.breadsoda.com, Su–Th noon–1:20AM, F–Sa noon–2:20AM)* welcomes with microbrews and robust sandwiches, plus billiards, ping-pong, darts, trivia, and more. For a well-rounded menu—from chicken pot pie to grilled salmon niçoise salad—and a tavernlike setting that incorporates leather booths, a mahogany bar, and white tablecloths, head to **Café Deluxe (23)** *(3228 Wisconsin Ave. NW, 202-686-2233, www.cafedeluxe.com, M–Th 11:30AM–10:30PM, F–Sa 11:30AM–11PM, Su 10:30AM–10PM)*. Everybody seems to be doing Prohibition-era cocktails; **Bourbon Glover Park (24)** *(2348 Wisconsin Ave., 202-625-7770, www.bourbondc.com, M–Th 5PM–2AM, F 5PM–3AM, Sa 11:30AM–3AM, Su 11:30AM–2AM)* does them better.

WHERE TO SHOP

For more than two decades, **Politics & Prose Bookstore and Coffeehouse (25)** *(5015 Connecticut Ave. NW, 202-364-1919 or 800-722-0790, www.politics-prose.com, M–Sa 9AM–10PM, Su 10AM–8PM)* has been the place to go for browsing, buying, and author events. Near the Friendship Heights Metro stop, you'll find a number of upscale shopping malls and freestanding stores, including **Mazza Gallerie (26)** *(5300 N. Wisconsin Ave. NW, 202-966-6114, www.mazzagallerie.com, M–F 10AM–8PM, Sa 10AM–7PM, Su noon–6PM)*, home to AMC theaters, Neiman Marcus, Pampillonia Jewelers, and

Oriental Decor. The **Chevy Chase Pavilion (27)** *(5335 Wisconsin Ave. NW, 202-207-3887, www.ccpavilion.com, M–Sa 10AM–8PM, Su noon–6PM)* across the street offers another collection of shops, including Pottery Barn, Stein Mart, Ann Taylor Loft, J. Crew, World  Market, and Alpaca International, which carries women's clothes from Europe and Peru. There is also a branch of the Parisian upscale contemporary furniture store **Roche Bobois (28)** *(Chevy Chase Plaza, 5301 Wisconsin Ave. NW, 202-686-5667, www.roche-bobois.com, M–Sa 10AM–6PM).* **Elizabeth Arden Salon (29)** *(5225 Wisconsin Ave. NW, 202-362-9890, www.red doorspas.com, M–Tu 8AM–7PM, W–Th 8AM–9PM, F–Sa 8AM–8PM, Su 9AM–6PM)* provides salon and spa services. For fashions with American style, shop **Lord & Taylor (30)** *(5255 Western Ave. NW, 202-362-9600, www.lordand taylor.com, M–Sa 10AM–9:30PM, Su 11AM–7PM).* Want something different? **Wake Up Little Suzie (31)** *(3409 Connecticut Ave. NW, 202-244-0700, http://wakeup littlesuzie.com/, M–Sa 11AM–6PM, Su noon–5PM)* is famous for its fun and fanciful gifts, including cat- and dog-shaped alarm clocks, unique pottery, and handcrafted jewelry.

WHERE TO STAY

One of the most elegant places to stay in the area is the **Omni Shoreham Hotel (32)** *($$-$$$)* *(2500 Calvert St. at Connecticut Ave. NW, 202-234-0700 or 888-444-6664, www.omnishorehamhotel.com).* The hotel is situated on

11 acres in Rock Creek Park; many of its rooms offer scenic views. The Omni has hosted inaugural balls for every administration since FDR. Bolder guests are known to book its "haunted ghost suite." The **Washington Marriott Wardman Park (33) ($$-$$$)** *(2660 Woodley Rd. NW, 202-328-2000 or 800-228-9290, www.marriott.com)*, the site of larger conventions, is set on a private 16-acre estate convenient to the Woodley Park-Zoo/Adams Morgan Metro stop. For a homey alternative to convention hotels, consider the **Woodley Park Guest House (34) ($$)** *(2647 Woodley Rd. NW, 202-667-0218 or 866-667-0218, www.woodleyparkguesthouse.com)*. This charming B&B is TV- and radio-free (though it does provide guest phones, voice mail, and high-speed Internet access). A generous "continental-plus" breakfast awaits you each morning. **Kalorama Guest House at Woodley Park (35) ($)** *(2700 Cathedral Ave. NW, 202-328-0860, www.kaloramaguesthouse.com)*, made up of two Victorian town houses, provides comfy accommodations at inviting prices. Continental breakfast is included. **Embassy Suites at Chevy Chase Pavilion (36) ($$)** *(Chevy Chase Pavilion, 4300 Military Rd. NW, www.embassysuitesdcmetro.com, 202-362-9300)* offers complimentary breakfast and has a fitness club and swimming pool.

ADAMS MORGAN

● *to Woodley Park-Zoo/Adams Morgan—to Metro bus*

● SNAPSHOT ●

Adams Morgan is one of the liveliest and most diverse neighborhoods in the Washington area. It's filled with edgy clubs, funky shops, and the famous colorful murals that brighten the façades of the buildings along Columbia Road and 18th Street. Adams Morgan attracts the young, the hip, and the adventurous, especially at night, when its clubs resonate with blues, jazz, rock, soul, bluegrass, and Latin music. International eateries abound: Choose from Mexican, Brazilian, Turkish, Italian, Middle Eastern, Ethiopian, French, Japanese, Vietnamese, El Salvadoran, Jewish, Greek, Pan Asian, Indian,  and all-American diner food, too. If avant-garde fashions, emerging designers, and offbeat furnishings intrigue you, you'll love Adams Morgan. You'll also like it if you're in search of something beyond official Washington. Stop by on the second Sunday in September, when the Adams Morgan Day Festival is in full swing. Artisans, food vendors, musicians, and dancers turn the area into a mélange of sights, scents, and flavors. Take the Metro here and walk across the Duke Ellington Bridge.

149

PLACES TO SEE

Arts & Entertainment:

Stroll from the Metro stop east into Adams Morgan; you'll feel the pulse of the neighborhood on Columbia Road and 18th Street NW. A walking tour of Adams Morgan murals will acquaint you with the history and culture of this unique community. The **Three Macaws Mural (37)** *(1706 Columbia Rd. NW)*, for example, is said to symbolize the neighborhood's ethnic diversity. Cultural diplomacy is alive and well in DC; the public performances and exhibits at the **Meridian International Center (38)** *(1630 Crescent Place NW, 202-667-6800, www.meridian. org)* strengthen international understanding. The popular **Cows on a Bicycle Mural (39)** *(2501 Champlain St. NW)*, by Sara Lee Terrat, sparked a community legal brouhaha some years ago. Adams Morgan is the heart of DC's Latino community. The **Mexican Cultural Institute (40)** *(2829 16th St. NW, 202-728-1647, M–F 10AM-6PM, Sa noon–4PM)* promotes Mexico's contemporary and traditional arts with a permanent gallery, film screenings, and discussions. The **Toulouse-Lautrec Mural (41)** *(2461 18th St. NW)* is a copy of the famed French artist's poster of cabaret singer Aristide Bruant. The eye-catching **Madam's Organ Mural (42)** *(2461 18th St. NW)* is perhaps the best-known—and most controversial—of the Adams Morgan public works of art. The **District of Columbia Arts Center (43)** *(2438 18th St. bet. Columbia/ Belmont Rds. NW, 202-462-7833, www.dcartscenter.org, W–Su 2PM–7PM)* provides a gallery and a 50-seat theater for emerging local, national, and international visual and performing artists. The **Champorama Park Mural (44)**

(corner of Champlain and Kalorama Rd. NW) was commissioned to revitalize an abandoned lot. A bench in this little pocket park provides a place for quiet reflection. Two blocks east you'll find a revitalized DC gem, the 12-acre **Meridian Hill Park (45)** *(2330 15th St. NW, 202-462-7275, www.nps.gov/mehi/, daily dawn–dusk)*, unofficially known as **Malcolm X Park**. It features a cascading water stairway, formal, Italian-style landscaping, and statues of Joan of Arc, Dante, and James Buchanan. Try to come late Sunday afternoon when the drum circle happens.

PLACES TO EAT & DRINK
Where to Eat:

Mama Ayesha's Restaurant (46) ($) *(1967 Calvert St. NW, 202-232-5431, www.mamaayeshas.com, Su–Th noon–9:30PM, F–Sa noon–10:30PM)* is a third-generation, family-owned institution serving Middle Eastern and Mediterranean food. Menu selections include Menzaleh, eggplant topped with ground beef, pine nuts, and tomato sauce. Or sample Mama's mezzes, including hummus, baba ghanoush, and tabbouleh.

For Ethiopian food, try **Meskerem (47) ($)** *(2434 18th St. NW, 202-462-4100, http://meskeremethiopianrestaurantdc.com/, M–Th 11AM–midnight, F–Su 11AM–2AM)*. Dishes are meant to be shared and eaten with fingers (no silverware here) over basketlike tables.

An excellent choice for Brazilian cuisine is **The Grill from Ipanema (48) ($$)** *(1858 Columbia Rd. NW, 202-986-0757, www.thegrilllfromipanema.com, M–Th 4:30PM–10:30PM, F 4:30PM–11:30PM, Su noon–10PM)*,  serving authentic dishes, from seafood stews with palm oil and coconut milk to marinated grilled fish, seared steaks, and garlic chicken, accompanied by cocktails made with cachaça, a white liquor distilled from sugarcane. For comfort food, **Cashion's Eat Place (49) ($$)** *(1819 Columbia Rd. NW, 202-797-1819, www.cashionseatplace.com, Tu 5:30PM–10PM, W–Sa 5:30PM–11PM, Su 11:30AM–2:30PM, 5:30PM–10PM)* can't be beat. Family photos line the walls and seasonal Southern-style fare with French and Italian influences draws enthusiastic diners. Sample selections include bison shoulder with red wine and rockfish over clam and celery root risotto. For flavorful regional Mexican cooking try **Mixtec (50) ($)** *(1792 Columbia Rd. NW, 202-332-1011, Su–Th 10AM–10PM, F–Sa 10AM–11PM)*, an informal café that's busy day and night. **Perry's (51) ($$)** *(1811 Columbia Rd. NW, 202-234-6218, www.perrysadamsmorgan.com, M–Th 5:30PM–10:30PM, F 5:30PM–11:30PM, Sa 11AM–3PM, 5:30PM–11:30PM, Su 10:30AM–2:30PM, 5:30PM–10:30PM)* pleases with American bistro and sushi selections and great views

from its rooftop dining room. The Sunday "drag" brunch is an award-winner. For generous helpings of great-tasting pasta, **Pasta Mia (52) ($)** *(1790 Columbia Rd. NW, 202-328-9114, Tu–Sa 6:30PM–10PM)* is the place. But be prepared to wait and bring cash—credit cards are not accepted here.

Bars & Nightlife:

Enjoy a dreamy evening at **Soussi (53)** *(2228 18th St. NW, 202-299-9313, www.soussiindc.com, M–Th 5PM–1AM, F–Sa 5PM–2AM, Su 5PM–midnight),* a hookah bar with a great outdoor patio. Strut your stuff at **Habana Village (54)** *(1834 Columbia Rd. NW, 202-462-6310, www.habana village.com, W–Sa 6:30PM–3AM, Su 4PM–midnight),* offering Cuban cuisine, Latin music, and weekly salsa/meringue lessons. Mojitos anyone? For blues, R&B, jazz, and authentic soul food, don't miss **Madam's Organ (55)** *(2461 18th St. NW, 202-667-5370, www.madams organ.com, M–Th 5PM–2AM, F–Sa 5PM–3AM, Su 5PM–2AM),* named one of the U.S.A.'s top bars by *Stuff* magazine. **Tryst Coffeehouse/Bar/Lounge (56)** *(2459 18th St. NW, 202-232-5500, www.trystdc.com, M–W 6:30AM–midnight, Th 6:30AM–2AM, F–Sa 6:30AM–3AM, Su 7AM–midnight)* is a hip place to have a sandwich or pastry, sip a latte or a Voodoo Lady (rum and hot vanilla chai), or check your e-mail (except weekends and holidays).

WHERE TO SHOP

Adams Morgan's international flavor translates into some of DC's most uncommon shopping experiences. For starters, browse the multilevel brownstone that houses **Skynear and Company (57)** *(2122 18th St. NW, 202-797-7160, www.skynearonline.com, M–Sa 11AM–7PM, Su noon–7PM)*. You'll find eclectic home furnishings from around the world. Upscale import store **Toro Mata (58)** *(2410 18th St. NW, 202-232-3890, http://www. toromata.com/portal/, Tu–F noon–8PM, Sa 10AM–8PM, Su noon–6PM)* specializes in ceramics, bold textiles, and hand-carved furniture from Peru. **Fleet Feet Sports (59)** *(1841 Columbia Rd. NW, 202-387-3888, www.fleet*  *feetdc.com, M–F 10AM–8PM, Sa 10AM–7PM, Su noon–4PM)* provides footwear and clothing for walkers, runners, and triathletes. It's easy for book lovers to be drawn into **Idle Time Books (60)** *(2467 18th St. NW, 202-232-4774, www.abebooks.com, daily 11AM–10PM)*. The comfortable two-story shop is chock-full of gently used and out-of-print books, CDs, and records. **Meeps (61)** *(2104 18th St. NW, 202-265-6546, www.meepsdc.com, M–Sa noon–7PM, Su noon–5PM)* is crammed with funky vintage used and new clothing and accessories for both men and women. The store likes to feature talented local designers, too.

WHERE TO STAY

Adam's Inn (62) ($) *(1746 Lanier Pl. NW, 202-745-3600 or 800-578-6807, www.adamsinn.com)*, located in three 100-year-old Victorian buildings on a residential street, is a bed-and-breakfast known for its comfort, charm, and affordability. **The Normandy Hotel (63) ($-$$)** *(2118 Wyoming Ave. NW, 202-483-1350, www.doylecollection.com)* offers Old World charm and well-appointed rooms. Enjoy tea and cookies served in the parlor every afternoon. **American Guest House (64) ($-$$)** *(2005 Columbia Rd. NW, 202-588-1180, www.americanguesthouse.com)*, an inn/B&B, is situated in a completely renovated 1889 home. Amenities include canopied beds, Wi-Fi Internet access, and full breakfast, including your choice of omelets and fresh fruit salad.

chapter 6

Places to See:

1. Dupont Memorial Fountain
2. Brewmaster's Castle
3. Patterson House
4. Woman's National Democratic Club
5. Anderson House
6. Townsend House
7. Spanish Steps
8. Phillips Collection
9. Textile Museum
10. Woodrow Wilson House
11. Fondo del Sol Visual Arts Center
12. National Museum of American Jewish Military History
13. Burton Marinkovich Fine Art
14. Charles Sumner School Museum and Archives
15. Theater J
16. Alliance Française de Washington
39. Duke Ellington Mural
40. Spirit of Freedom Sculpture
41. African American Civil War Memorial Freedom Foundation and Museum
42. Thurgood Marshall Center for Service and Heritage
43. Mary McLeod Bethune Council House National Historic Site
44. Lincoln Theatre
45. Hamiltonian Gallery
46. Studio Theatre
71. Catholic University of America
72. Trinity Washington University
73. Basilica of the National Shrine of the Immaculate Conception
74. Pope John Paul II Cultural Center
75. Mount St. Sepulchre Franciscan Monastery
76. National Arboretum

157

Places to Eat & Drink:

17. Obelisk
18. Al Tiramisu
19. Lauriol Plaza
20. Kramerbooks & Afterwords Café & Grill
21. Komi
22. Restaurant Nora
23. Firefly
24. The Big Hunt
25. Eighteenth Street Lounge
26. Veritas Wine Bar
27. Fox and Hounds Lounge
47. Busboys and Poets
48. Café Saint-Ex
49. Ben's Chili Bowl
50. Logan Tavern
51. Commissary DC
52. Etete
53. Gate 54
54. Black Cat
55. The Gibson
56. Bohemian Caverns

Where to Shop:

28. Proper Topper
29. Books-A-Million
30. Second Story Books
31. Beadazzled
32. Secondi
57. Pulp
58. Lettie Gooch Boutique
59. Home Rule
60. Vastu
61. Muléh
62. Shoefly
63. GoodWood
64. Habitat Live and Wear
65. Hemphill Fine Arts
66. Reincarnations

Where to Stay:

33. Hotel Madera
34. Dupont Circle Hotel
35. The Fairfax at Embassy Row
36. The Churchill Hotel
37. Hilton Washington
38. Hotel Tabard Inn
67. Hotel Rouge
68. Hotel Helix
69. DC GuestHouse
70. Donovan House

⬤ *to Dupont Circle*

• SNAPSHOT •

Dupont Circle is a cosmopolitan neighborhood that bustles with activity, drawing people of all types to its restaurants, bookstores, museums, coffee bars, and chess tables. The traffic circle itself is ideal for people-watching. Dupont Circle has grown from rural Civil War–era roots, when it began to welcome prominent people from throughout the city and the nation. These days, embassies, social clubs, private offices, think tanks, and other institutions fill the neighborhood's mansions, and Dupont Circle draws those seeking an international urban flavor and diversity, including gays, lesbians, and bisexuals. It also offers some of the city's best museums and art galleries. Kalorama is an elegant private neighborhood that harbors five presidential homes. Its northwestern boundaries are defined by Rock Creek.

159

PLACES TO SEE
Landmarks:

Start at the **Dupont Memorial Fountain (1)** *(Dupont Circle)*, named in honor of Samuel Francis Dupont, a Civil War

naval hero. Three figures representing the Arts of Ocean Navigation—the Sea, the Wind, and the Stars—decorate the base. Just south of the circle on Sunderland Place, you'll spot the wrought-iron fence of the **Brewmaster's Castle (2)** *(1307 New Hampshire Ave. NW, 202-429-1894, www.heurichhouse.org, tours W by appt; tours Th–F 11:30AM, 1PM, Sa 11:30AM, 1PM, 2:30PM)*. The house was built between 1892 and 1894 for brewery owner Christian Heurich. It's considered one of America's most intact late-Victorian homes, and an early "smart house"—with fireproofing, full plumbing, hot water, a central vac system, and more. The nearby **Patterson House (3)** *(15 Dupont Circle, 202-483-9200, www.thewashington club.com)*, a Beaux-Arts mansion, was designed by Stanford White; it was the residence of the Calvin Coolidges in 1927 while the White House was undergoing repairs. Named for its original owner, Robert Patterson of Chicago, editor of the *Chicago Tribune*, and his wife, Elizabeth Medill Patterson, it was the setting for elaborate parties. Now called the **Washington Club**, it's home to a private social club. **Woman's National Democratic Club (4)** *(1526 New Hampshire Ave., 202-232-7363, www.democraticwoman.org; tours by appt)* has its home in the Whittemore House, named after opera singer Sarah Adams Whittemore, a descendant of

President John Adams. The home exudes a fairy-tale look with its English slate roof, leaded glass windows, and turrets. Massachusetts Ave. west of Sheridan Circle is known as **Embassy Row** for the many embassies now housed in its stately mansions. Follow the circle around to Massachusetts Ave. heading northwest to the **Anderson House (5)** *(2118 Massachusetts Ave. NW, 202-785-2040, open Tu–Sa 1PM–4PM, www.societyofthecincinnati.org)*, an Italianate palace built for career diplomat Larz Anderson III and his wife, Isabel Weld Perkins. Today it serves as

headquarters for the Society of the Cincinnati, a benevolent organization established by George Washington for his officers and their direct descendants. It also has a collection of decorative and fine arts and Revolutionary War artifacts. The **Townsend House (6)** *(2121 Massachusetts Ave. NW, 202-387-7783, www.cosmosclub.org)* across the street was built in 1901 for railroad magnate Richard Townsend; it's now home to the Cosmos Club, a private club dedicated to the advancement of its members in science, literature, and art. Past Sheridan Circle, Massachusetts intersects with S Street. Turn right and continue east until you reach 22nd Street. Make another right, where you will see an unmarked dead end. Walk to the end to see Washington's version of Rome's **Spanish Steps (7)**; they once led to an 18th-century manor house called Kalorama, Greek for "beautiful view."

Arts & Entertainment:

The neighborhood boasts a variety of specialty museums, mostly situated north of the circle on R and S Streets. Don't miss the **Phillips Collection (8)** *(1600 21st St. NW, 202-387-2151, www.phillipscollection.org, Tu–W 10AM–5PM, Th 10AM–8:30PM, F–Sa 10AM–5PM, Su 11AM–6PM)*, the first modern art museum in the country. With nearly 2,500 works by American and European impressionists and modern artists, it is considered one of the world's

finest small museums. It is home to Renoir's renowned *Luncheon of the Boating Party*, works by El Greco, van Gogh, Degas, Cézanne, Matisse, Monet, de Kooning, Hopper, and O'Keeffe. The museum also hosts a popular Sunday afternoon concert series from October through May. If textiles tickle your fancy, follow Massachusetts Ave. past Sheridan Circle to the **Textile Museum (9)** *(2320 S St. NW, 202-667-0441, www.textilemuseum.org, Tu–Sa 10AM–5PM, Su 1PM–5PM)*, where 17,000 tapestries, carpets, clothing, and more, dating from 3,000 B.C. to the present, await. Learn through exhibits and a hands-on center that focuses on Oriental carpets and weavings from the Old World and New World, as well as pre-Columbian, Peruvian, and Islamic works. The **Woodrow Wilson House (10)** *(2340 S St. NW, 202-387-4062, www.woodrowwilsonhouse.org, Tu–Su 10AM–4PM)* is the only presidential museum in the city. Wilson's final home

after his presidency, it depicts the 28th president's life and times through objects, furnishings, recordings, and silent films. **Fondo del Sol Visual Arts Center (11)** *(2112 R St. NW, 202-483-2777, www.dkmuseums.com/fondo.html, W–Sa 1PM–6PM)* devotes itself to the art, music, and culture of Latin, Caribbean, Native-American, and African-American peoples in Washington through exhibits, concerts, lectures, and poetry readings. Learn about the contributions of Jewish Americans in the U.S. Armed Services at the **National Museum of American Jewish Military History (12)** *(1811 R St. NW, 202-265-6280, www.nmajmh.org, M–F 9AM–5PM)*. You can view documents, medals, memorabilia, and firearms from American military conflicts. Walking west, you'll discover a gem of an art gallery. **Burton Marinkovich Fine Art (13)** *(1506 21st St. NW, 202-296-6563, www.burtonmarinkovich.com, Tu–Sa 11AM–6PM)* displays prints, drawings, and paintings by modern and contemporary masters, such as Joan Miró and Alexander Calder. Learn more about local history at the **Charles Sumner School Museum and Archives (14)** *(1201 17th St. NW, 202-442-6060, M–Sa 10AM–5PM)*, site of the first public school for African-American students in Washington, and former headquarters for the superintendent and board of trustees for Colored Public Schools of Washington and Georgetown. East of Dupont Circle is progressive **Theater J (15)** *(Washington, DC Jewish Community Center, 1529 16th St. NW, 800-494-8497, www.dcjcc.org/arts/theater, box office, 1 hour prior to performance)*; it's received numerous Helen

Hayes Award nominations. For a range of courses, social activities, and cultural events pertaining to France, **Alliance Française de Washington (16)** *(2142 Wyoming Ave. NW, 202-234-7911, www.francedc.org, M–F 10AM–6PM, Sa 10AM–4PM)* is the place.

PLACES TO EAT & DRINK
Where to Eat:

Dupont Circle has more restaurants per block than almost any other Washington neighborhood. Here is a sampling of choices in a variety of atmospheres. For refined Italian, consider **Obelisk (17) ($$$)** *(2029 P St. NW, 202-872-1180, Tu–Sa 6PM–10PM)* and its prix fixe five-course dinner (reserve well in advance). **Al Tiramisu (18) ($$-$$$)** *(2014 P St. NW, 202-467-4466, www.altiramisu.com, M–F noon–2:30PM, 5:30PM–10:30PM, Sa 5:30PM–10:30PM, Su 5PM–9:30PM)*, another authentic Italian eatery, imports 90 percent of its ingredients and all of its seafood and wine from Italy. You'll enjoy its friendly neighborhood feel. The risotto of the day is always a good choice. Lively ambience combines with moderately priced Mexican/Spanish food and refreshing margaritas at **Lauriol Plaza (19) ($)** *(1835 18th St. NW, 202-387-0035, www.lauriol*

plaza.com, Su–Th 11:30AM–11:30PM, F–Sa 11:30AM–midnight). Try *zarzuela de mariscos*, a seafood casserole of scallops, shrimp, fresh fish, squid, mussels, and clams, or *bistec a la criolla*, mesquite-grilled New York sirloin with sautéed Spanish onions.

Kramerbooks & Afterwords Café & Grill (20) ($) *(1517 Connecticut Ave. NW, 202-387-3825, www.kramers.com, Su–Th 7:30AM–1AM, F–Sa open 24 hours)* has been a DC institution since 1976. The bookstore café is perfect for a quick bite, coffee, or a full meal. Enjoy live music  Wednesday through Saturday nights. Late, late night everyone comes for Southern desserts—peach cobbler and pecan pie. At **Komi (21) ($$$)** *(1509 17th St. NW, 202-332-9200, www.komirestaurant.com, Tu–Sa 5:30PM–9:30PM)* the creative Greek-inspired prix fixe menu offers diners an unparalleled gustatory experience. It's a tiny space; reservations are essential. **Restaurant Nora (22)** *(2132 Florida Ave. NW, 202-462-5143, www.noras.com, M–Th 5:30PM–10PM, F–Sa 5:30PM–10:30PM)* serves organic, seasonal new-American cuisine. The walls are bedecked with Amish quilts, giving the dining room a warm, inviting feel. A block and a half off Dupont Circle, you'll find **Firefly (23) ($-$$)** *(Hotel Madera, 1310 New Hampshire Ave. NW, 202-861-1310, www.firefly-dc.com, M–Th 7AM–10AM, 11:30AM–2PM, 5:30PM–10PM, F 7AM–10AM, 11:30AM–2PM, 5:30PM–10:30PM, Sa 9AM–2PM, 5:30PM–10:30PM, Su 9AM–2PM, 5:30PM–10PM)*, where tiny lanterns dangle from a faux tree and diners enjoy innovative American food, like "corned" pork tenderloin with butternut squash dumplings, or jumbo lump crab cakes with roasted poblano aioli.

Bars & Nightlife:

The Big Hunt (24) *(1345 Connecticut Ave. NW, 202-785-2333, www.thebighunt.net, M–Th 4PM–2AM, F–Sa 4PM–3AM, Su 5PM–2AM)*

draws regulars and newcomers to its laid-back, split-level bar. It features Internet jukeboxes, pool tables, and a plethora of TV screens. Swanky **Eighteenth Street Lounge (25)** *(1212 18th St. NW, 202-466-3922, www.eighteenth streetlounge.com, Tu–Th 5:30PM–2AM, F 5:30PM–3AM, Sa 9:30PM–3AM, Su 9:30PM–2AM)* is a bar-lounge-club with a mellow, mature crowd that sips champagne while listening to an eclectic selection of live music and DJ mix sets. Ultra-chic **Veritas Wine Bar (26)** *(2031 Florida Ave., NW, 202-265-6270, www.veritasdc.com, daily 5PM–1AM)* offers a wide spectrum of wines—more than 70 by the glass—paired with simple, shareable plates of cheese and charcuterie. **Fox and Hounds Lounge (27)** *(1537 17th St. NW, 202-232-6307, www.triofoxand hounds.com, Su–Th 11AM–2AM, F–Sa 11AM–3AM)* has an unpretentious clientele, and, patrons say, some of the strongest mixed drinks in DC. Its outdoor patio is perfect for people watching.

WHERE TO SHOP

Proper Topper (28) *(1350 Connecticut Ave. NW, 202-842-3055, www.propertopper.com, M–F 10AM–8PM, Sa 10AM–7PM, Su noon–6PM)* will win you over with its whimsical hats, jewelry, purses, pretty dresses, and casual wear. You'll find kids' stuff and gifts too. Shelves of the latest bestsellers abound at **Books-A-Million (29)** *(11 Dupont Cir., 202-319-1374, www.booksamillion.com, M–Sa 9AM–11PM, Su 9AM–9PM)*, or browse used and rare books, LP records, CDs, and DVDs at **Second Story Books (30)** *(2000 P St. NW, 202-659-8884, www.secondstorybooks.com, daily 10AM–10PM)*. **Beadazzled (31)** *(1507 Connecticut Ave. NW, 202-265-2323, www.beadazzled.net, M–Sa 10AM–8PM, Su 11AM–6PM)* offers an amazing array of loose beads (glass, wood, shell, copper, silver, and gold) seed beads, pearl and gemstone beads, and art glass. They also sell all the tools and equipment you need to finish your bead projects. **Secondi (32)** *(1702 Connecticut Ave. NW, 2nd fl., 202-667-1122, www.secondi.com, M–Tu 11AM–6PM, W–F 11AM–7PM, Sa 11AM–6PM, Su 1PM–5PM)* is a consignment shop that carries "good as new" designer fashions for women, including Chanel, Vuitton, Prada, and more.

WHERE TO STAY

For chic, contemporary accommodations, complete with coffeemakers with Starbucks coffee, animal-print robes, and Aveda bath products, you'll feel right at home at **Hotel Madera (33) ($$)** *(1310 New Hampshire Ave. NW, 202-296-7600 or 800-368-5691, www.hotelmadera.com)*. It's just a block and a half from the circle itself. Cardio rooms—with treadmills or exercise bikes—are available on request. Guests at the sleek boutique **Dupont Circle Hotel (34) ($$-$$$)** *(1500 New Hampshire St. NW, 202-483-6000, www.doylecollection.com)* enjoy lavishly styled rooms with heated bathroom floors and luxe linens. The lively location on Dupont Circle is part of the experience. The recently restored **Fairfax at Embassy Row (35) ($$$)** *(2100 Massachusetts Ave. NW, 202-293-2100, www.starwood hotels.com)* boasts superb comfort, including custom beds and baths and a fitness center. The hotel was the childhood home of Al Gore when his father, the late Al Gore Sr., was a senator. Another option a little farther from the heart of Dupont Circle is **The Churchill Hotel (36) ($$-$$$)** *(1914 Connecticut Ave. NW, 202-797-2000 or 800-424-2464, www.thechurchillhotel.com)*, a Beaux-Arts gem where historic elegance, spacious rooms, and modern amenities mix. The legendary **Hilton Washington (37) ($$-$$$)** *(1919 Connecticut Ave. NW, 202-483-3000 or 800-HILTONS, www.washington. hilton.com)* is a huge 1,000-room-plus resort, offering landscaped gardens and an Olympic pool. It's sometimes referred to as the "Reagan Hilton," because president Reagan was shot and wounded outside the hotel in 1981. The Victorian **Hotel Tabard Inn (38) ($-$$)** *(1739 N St. NW, 202-785-1277, www.tabardinn.com)* has 40 individually furnished rooms, some with private bath, some not. This popular inn does not have an elevator or televisions in its rooms, though it does provide other modern comforts, including Wi-Fi. Enjoy live jazz in the lounge on Sunday evenings.

● to Mount Vernon Square/
7th Street-Convention Center, or U Street/African-
American Civil War Memorial/Cardozo

● to Farragut North

●● to McPherson Square

● SNAPSHOT ●

Nearly destroyed after the riots that followed the assassination of Martin Luther King, Jr., the U Street area, the soul of Washington's African-American community, has been revitalized and is now emerging as one of the most vibrant neighborhoods in the Capital City. U Street was home to jazz great Duke Ellington and poet Langston Hughes. "Black Broadway" nightclub-goers enjoyed performances by Pearl Bailey, Louis Armstrong, Cab Calloway, Lionel Hampton, Ella Fitzgerald, Billy Eckstine, Billie Holiday, and Sarah Vaughan, among others. Today, the neighborhood's historic Lincoln Theatre is home to jazz, comedy, poetry, and dance. With the opening of new clubs and restaurants, U Street and the adjacent area surrounding stately Logan Circle draw locals and visitors alike.

PLACES TO SEE
Landmarks:

One of the first things you'll see if you arrive by Metro at the U Street/African-American Civil War Memorial stop is the **Duke Ellington Mural (39)** *(1200 U St. NW, True Reformer Building)*, by G. Byron Peck; it's a 24-by 32-foot likeness of the jazz legend surveying the scene. The mural is an ever-present reminder of Ellington's impact on the neighborhood in its heyday during the first half of the 20th century. If you exit the Metro at Vermont Avenue, you'll see Ed Hamilton's **Spirit of Freedom Sculpture (40)** *(1000 U St. NW)* dedicated to black Civil War troops. Learn about their fight for freedom through photos and documents at the **African American Civil War Memorial Freedom Foundation and Museum (41)** *(1200 U St. NW, 202-667-2667, www.afroamcivilwar.org, M–F 10AM–5PM, Sa 10AM–2PM)*. Walking southwest to 12th Street, you'll pass the **Thurgood Marshall Center for Service and Heritage (42)** *(Twelfth Street/Anthony Bowen YMCA, 1816 12th St. NW, 202-462-8314, www.thurgoodmarshallcenter.org)*, named for Thurgood Marshall, grandson of a slave, chief counsel for the NAACP, and supreme court justice. Check out the museum on the first floor to learn more about the community and its famous residents, including Langston Hughes and Duke Ellington. Farther south, Vermont Avenue, Rhode Island Avenue, and P Street intersect at Logan Circle. If you walk southwest on Vermont, you'll come across the **Mary McLeod Bethune Council House National Historic Site (43)** *(1318 Vermont Ave. NW, 202-673-2402, www.nps.gov/mamc, M–Sa 9AM–5PM)*. Bethune, a daughter of former slaves, was founder of the National Council of Negro Women and an advisor to four presidents on African-American issues. This Victorian house was council headquarters and her home from 1943 to 1949.  The house is now a museum and home of the National Archives for Black Women's History.

Arts & Entertainment:

Near the Metro stop, you'll see the fabled **Lincoln Theatre (44)** *(1215 U St. bet. 12th/13th Sts. NW, 202-328-6000, www.thelincolntheatre.org, box office M–F 10AM–6PM)*, the 1920s venue that hosted myriad black music greats, now restored to its original glory. Public performances and private events, ranging from jazz concerts to poetry contests to school graduations, take place here today. **Hamiltonian Gallery (45)** *(1353 U St. NW, 202-332-1116, www.hamiltoniangallery.com, Tu–Sa noon–6PM)* tends toward experimental sculpture, paintings, and photographs from regional artists. Artist-founded and artist-driven **Studio Theatre (46)** *(1501 14th St. NW, 202-332-3300, www.studiotheatre. org, box office W–F 10AM–7PM, Sa 10AM–1PM and 3PM–7PM, Su noon–1PM and 3PM–6PM)* offers contemporary, edgy theater productions.

PLACES TO EAT & DRINK
Where to Eat:

A steady stream of the intelligentsia frequent **Busboys & Poets (47) ($)** *(2021 14th St. NW, 202-387-7638, Su 9AM–midnight, M–Th 8AM–midnight, F 8AM–2AM, Sa 9AM–2AM)* to have a bite to eat, linger over coffee, or attend one of the store's many lectures, film screenings, or open mic poetry events. This unique bookstore café's menu features specialties as varied as coconut tofu bites with plum sauce, *mekhleme* (Iraqi "corned" beef hash), and French toast. The menu at aviation-themed **Café Saint-Ex (48) ($)** *(1847 14th St. NW, 202-265-7839, www.saint-ex.com, M 5PM–1:30AM, Tu–Th 11AM–1:30AM, F–Sa 11AM–2:30AM, Su 11AM–1:30AM)*—named after French aviator/author Antoine de Saint-Exupery—includes sustainable, organic, and fresh local items when possible.

 Sample wild mushroom risotto, bistro-style seared mussels, or a pint of specialty beer or ale. Follow in the footsteps of Duke Ellington, Ella Fitzgerald, and Martin Luther King, Jr. and experience authentic U Street at **Ben's Chili Bowl (49) ($)** *(1213 U St. NW, 202-667-0909, www.benschilibowl.com, M–Th 6AM–2AM, F 6AM–4AM, Sa 7AM–4AM, Su 11AM–11PM)*. Drawing crowds since 1958, Ben's is the place for classic chili con carne (or the vegetarian version), homemade potato salad, and cheese fries. Try the chili half-smoke, Bill Cosby's favorite. For a laid-back bar-and-grill vibe with a local following, try **Logan Tavern (50) ($-$$)** *(1423 P St. NW, 202-332-3710, www.logantavern.com, M–Tu noon–11PM, F noon–midnight,*

Sa 11AM–midnight, Su 11AM–10:30PM). Menu options include mixed greens and jicama salad, wasabi-crusted meat loaf, grilled tuna or salmon, and grilled turkey steak in maple and citrus. **Commissary DC (51) ($-$$)** *(1443 P St. NW, 202-299-0018, www.commissarydc.com, M–Th 8AM–11PM, F 8AM–midnight, Sa 9AM–midnight, Su 9PM–11PM)*, a neighborhood mainstay, serves up giant helpings of all-day breakfast and uncomplicated lunch and dinner choices, like tuna melts and chicken fried steak. For authentic Ethiopian fare, **Etete (52) ($)** *(1942 9th St. NW, 202-232-7600, www.eteterestaurant.com, daily 11AM–1AM)* fills the bill. Its sambusas—lentils cooked in pastry—are excellent. Eating without utensils is all part of the experience.

Bars & Nightlife:

Gate 54 (53) *(1847 14th St. NW, 202-265-7839, www.saint-ex.com, M 5PM–1:30AM, Tu–Th 11AM–1:30AM, F–Sa 11AM–2:30AM, Su 11AM–1:30AM)* located downstairs in the **Café Saint-Ex (48)**, is a hip spot to have a drink and listen to DJs in an airplane hangar-inspired lounge. Rock out to alternative and independent live music at **Black Cat (54)** *(1811 14th St. NW, 202-667-7960, www.blackcatdc.com, Su–Th 8PM–2AM, F–Sa 7PM–3AM)*. You can also order a beer, a Texas veggie burger, listen to a poem, or relax in the club's no-cover Red Room Bar, where you can play pinball or pool. Dimly lit and semi-secret, **The Gibson (55)** *(2009 14th St. NW, 202-232-2156, www.thegibsondc.com, Su–Th 6PM–1AM, F–Sa 6PM–2AM)* is a speakeasy style bar.

Weekend reservations are a must. Originally founded in the 1920s as Club Caverns, **Bohemian Caverns (56)** *(2003 11th St. NW, 202-299-0800, www.bohemian caverns.com, M 6PM–midnight, Th–Sa 8PM–1AM)* showcases local jazz talent in its cozy subterranean space.

WHERE TO SHOP

U Street shoppers tend to favor the offbeat, the unique, and the unconventional. The U Street Metro stop on the Green Line includes **Pulp (57)** *(1803 14th St. NW, 202-462-7857, www.pulpdc.com, M–Sa 11AM–7PM, Su 11AM–5PM)*, the destination for out-of-the-ordinary greeting cards, gifts, and stationery. Come to **Lettie Gooch Boutique (58)** *(1517 U St. NW, 202-332-4242, www.lettiegooch.com, M–Sa noon–7PM, Su noon–5PM)* for the perfect party dress or designer casual wear. **Home Rule (59)** *(1807* *14th St. NW, 202-797-5544, www.homerule.com, M–Sa 11AM– 7PM, Su noon–5:30PM)* stocks whimsical oven mitts, magnetic spice racks, illuminated ice cubes, and kid-friendly flatware. For more home designs, stop at **Vastu (60)** *(1829 14th St. NW, 202-234-8344, www.vastudc.com, Tu–Sa 11AM– 7PM, Su noon–5PM)*, which takes its name from the Sanskrit belief that the arrangement of household objects promotes well-being. Browse its intriguing collection of custom-designed sofas, resin vases, and hardwood lamps. For Asian-inspired home furnishings and trendy women's wear, **Muléh (61)** *(1831 14th St. NW, 202-667-3440, www.muleh.com, M–Sa 11AM–7PM, Su noon–5PM)* is a must. Cute, affordable shoes and handbags draw the fashionable to **ShoeFly (62)** *(1520 U St. NW, 202-332-1077, www.shoeflyonline. com, M–F noon–7PM, Sa 11AM–6PM, Su noon–5PM).* You'll find jewelry too. For 19th-century American antiques, decorative arts, pottery, and lamps visit **GoodWood (63)** *(1428 U St. NW, 202-986-3640, www.goodwooddc.com, W–Sa noon–7PM, Su noon–5PM).* Contemporary handcrafted jewelry and accessories fill the displays at **Habitat Live and Wear (64)** *(1510 U St. NW, 202-518-7222, www.habitatstyle.com, M–Tu and Th–F 11:30AM–7PM, Sa–Su noon–6PM).* **Hemphill Fine Arts (65)** *(1515 14th St. NW, 202-234-5601, www. hemphillfinearts.com, Tu–Sa 10AM–5PM)* shows the work of nationally recognized and emerging artists. For a mix of new and used furniture and accessories, stop by **Reincarnations (66)** *(1401 14th St. NW, 202-319-1606, www.reincarnations.com, Tu–Su 11AM–8PM).*

WHERE TO STAY

Hotel Rouge (67) ($$) *(1315 16th St. NW, 202-232-8000 or 800-368-5689, www.rougehotel.com)* is a deluxe boutique hotel in Scott Circle, three blocks from Logan Circle. Amenities include 37-inch high-def TVs, down comforters, and evening wine receptions. Want to be closer to U Street/Logan Circle? Stay at hip **Hotel Helix (68) ($$)** *(1430 Rhode Island Ave. NW, 202-462-9001 or 800-706-1202, www.hotelhelix.com)*, offering an array of unique amenities. Charming bed and breakfast **DC GuestHouse (69) ($$)** *(1337 10th St. NW, 202-332-2502, www.dcguesthouse.com)*, a historic mansion one block

from the convention center, features six spacious guest rooms decorated with art and furnishings from all over the world. It also offers a handy business center. You'll enjoy the tasty full breakfast. The **Donovan House (70)** *(1155 14th St. NW, 202-737-1200, www.donovanhousedc.com)* has

lavishly appointed rooms complete with 400-thread count linens and cocoon spiral showers.

BROOKLAND

● *to Brookland-CUA*

East of U Street is an outlying neighborhood called Brookland, situated around the Brookland/CUA Metro stop on the Red Line. Dubbed "Little Rome," it is home to the largest number of Catholic institutions (nearly 60) outside the Vatican. You'll find the **Catholic University of America (71)** *(620 Michigan Ave. NE, 202-319-5000, www.cua.edu)*; **Trinity Washington University (72)** *(125 Michigan Ave. NE, 202-884-9000, www.trinitydc.edu)*; the **Basilica of the National Shrine of the Immaculate Conception (73)** *(400 Michigan Ave. NE, 202-526-8300, www.nationalshrine.com)*, which is the largest Catholic Church in the U.S.; the **Pope John Paul II Cultural Center (74)** *(3900 Harwood Rd. NE, 202-635-5400, www.jp2cc.org)*; and the **Mount St. Sepulchre Franciscan Monastery (75)**, *(1400 Quincy St. NE, 202-526-6800, www.myfranciscan.com)*, offering 40 landscaped acres with replicas of famous gardens and shrines from the Holy Land. The African-American community also made this area home in the 1930s. Notable residents included Nobel Laureate Ralph Bunche and Pearl Bailey. The nearby **National Arboretum (76)** *(3501 New York Ave. NE, 202-245-2726, www.usna.usda.gov, 8AM–5PM)*, a 444-acre sanctuary, features the National Bonsai and Penjing Museum and the National Herb Garden.

chapter 7

SOUTHWEST WATERFRONT

ANACOSTIA

Places to See:

1. Titanic Memorial
2. Fort Lesley J. McNair
3. Thomas Law House
4. Wheat Row
5. St. Dominic's Church
6. Benjamin Banneker Park
7. Odyssey
8. Spirit Cruises
9. Arena Stage
10. Washington Navy Yard
26. Frederick Douglass National Historic Site
27. Fort Stanton and Washington Overlook
28. Fort Dupont Park
29. Anacostia Museum
30. Anacostia Park
31. Kenilworth Park and Aquatic Gardens

Places to Eat & Drink:

11. CityZen
12. Sou'Wester
13. Phillips Flagship
14. Pier 7
15. Jenny's Asian Fusion
16. Cantina Marina
17. Next Stage by José Andrés Catering with Ridgewells
18. Bar at CityZen
19. Empress Lounge

Where to Shop:

20. Maine Avenue Fish Wharf

Where to Stay:

21. Channel Inn
22. L'Enfant Plaza Hotel
23. Mandarin Oriental Hotel
24. Residence Inn Marriott Washington, DC/Capitol
25. Capitol Skyline Hotel

⬤⬤⬤⬤ *to L'Enfant Plaza*

⬤⬤ *to Federal Center SW*

⬤ *to Waterfront-SEU, or Navy Yard*

• SNAPSHOT •

Just south of the Washington Mall you'll find **L'Enfant Plaza**. Further south is the neighborhood known as Southwest Waterfront. A former working-class, immigrant neighborhood revitalized in the fifties, the area was part of the Underground Railroad, and home of Al Jolson. One of its chief landmarks is Arena Stage, established in 1950, now a three-theater complex, including a Tony Award-winning resident theater. One of the attractions of the Southwest Waterfront neighborhood is, naturally, its proximity to the water. The Washington Channel—between East Potomac Park and the neighborhood itself—is filled with sailboats, yachts, fishing boats, and cruise tour boats. Though Capitol Hill is close at hand, it seems far away from this self-contained waterfront neighborhood.

PLACES TO SEE
Landmarks:

Most of the buildings in this area house federal agencies, such as the Federal Aviation Administration, the Department of Education, the Department of Agriculture, and the Department of Health and Human Services; these are not open to tourists. To reach the waterfront, take the Green Line to Waterfront-SEU. At the end of the promenade near the **Washington Channel** is a small park that serves as the backdrop for the **Titanic Memorial (1)** *(4th and P Sts. SW)*, a sculpture dedicated to the men who died in the *Titanic* shipwreck in 1912 trying to save the lives of women and children. Farther south along the channel is **Fort Lesley J. McNair (2)** *(4th and P Sts. SW)*. More than two centuries old, it was built to defend the capital city at Greenleaf Point, where the Potomac River and the Anacostia meet. This was also the site where Lincoln assassination conspirators were tried and hanged. The **Thomas Law House (3)** *(1252 6th St. SW)*, built in 1796, is a three-story Federal-style house, first occupied by Thomas Law and his wife, Elizabeth Custis, a granddaughter of Martha Washington. Renovated in 1965, it now serves as the community center for Tiber Island residents. Although it is not open to the public, it can be rented out for special events. Nearby historic **Wheat Row (4)** *(1315–21 4th St. SW)*, built in 1795, contains some of the earliest row houses built in DC. Walking

north, you'll see **St. Dominic's Church (5)** *(630 E St. SW)*, a Gothic landmark dating from 1875, known for its stained-glass windows and 250-foot steeple. **Benjamin Banneker Park (6)** *(10th and G Sts. SW)* memorializes the scientist hired by George Washington to assist in the surveying of the area that would become the District of Columbia.

Arts & Entertainment:

For an experience that will appeal to all of your senses,

sail on the **Odyssey (7)** *(Gangplank Marina, 600 Water St. SW, 866-306-2469, www.odysseycruises.com)*, where you will cruise on the Potomac River, eat a sumptuous meal, and listen and dance to live music. Another dining/entertainment cruise line is **Spirit Cruises (8)** *(Pier 4, 6th and Water Sts. SW, 202-554-8013 or 866-211-3811, www.spiritcruises.com)*, which offers lunch, dinner/dance, and moonlight cruise options. Sail on their *Spirit of Mount Vernon*, which will take you to Mount Vernon, George Washington's home. Easily accessible from the Waterfront-SEU Metro stop, award-winning **Arena Stage (9)** *(1101 6th St. SW, 202-488-3300, www.arenastage.org)*, DC's largest nonprofit theater, produces classic American dramas, comedies, and musicals, as well as new plays and works in progress. The stunning Mead Center for American Theater, which opened in October 2010, is Arena's new state-of-the art performance facility. For a change of pace, take the Metro to the **Washington Navy Yard (10)** *(9th and M Sts.).*

This area served as the Naval gun factory during the 19th century. Visit the **Navy Museum** *(805 Kidder Breese SE, 202-433-6826, www.history.navy.mil, M–F 9AM–5PM, Sa–Su 10AM–5PM)*. It spans more than 200 years of naval history, and showcases weapons and battles from the Revolutionary War through contemporary conflicts. Next door to the Navy Museum is the **USS *Barry*** *(M–F 9AM–5PM, Sa–Su 10AM–5PM)*, a Cold War-era destroyer ship you can tour.

PLACES TO EAT & DRINK
Where to Eat:

Named one of the "Hottest Restaurants in the World" by *Food & Wine*, **CityZen (11) ($$$)** *(Mandarin Oriental Hotel, 1330 Maryland Ave. SW, 202-787-6006, www.mandarinoriental.com/washington, Tu–Th 6PM–9:30PM, F–Sa 5:30PM–11:30PM)* provides the perfect special-occasion dining experience. The decor artfully combines elements of wood, water, fire, earth, and metal. Enjoy a drink as you watch the activity in the exhibition kitchen. Three menu variations are offered: a three-course prix fixe, a six-course chef's tasting menu, and a six-course vegetarian menu. CityZen also boasts a single malt whisky collection, rare cognacs, and a wine cellar with over 500 selections. For high-end Southern comfort food and spectacular Potomac views, choose **Sou'Wester (12) ($$)** *(Mandarin Oriental Hotel, 1330 Maryland Ave. SW, 202-767-6868, www.mandarinoriental.com/washington, daily 6:30AM–10PM)*, the Mandarin Oriental Hotel's less formal restaurant. **Phillips Flagship (13) ($$)** *(900 Water St. SW,*

202-488-8515, *www.phillipsseafood.com/phillipsflagship,
Su–Th 11AM–9PM, F–Sa 11AM–10PM*) tempts with its
bountiful all-you-can-eat seafood buffet, sushi bar,
traditional menu, and water views. Great seafood and
views can also be found at **Pier 7 (14) ($$)** (*650 Water
St. SW, 202-554-2500, www.pier7restaurant.com, daily
11AM–3PM, 5PM–10PM*), the oldest family-owned and
operated restaurant on the waterfront. **Jenny's Asian
Fusion (15) ($-$$)** (*1000 Water St. SW, 202-554-2202,
www.jennysdc.com, M–Th 11AM–10PM, F–Sa 11AM–
11PM, Su noon–10PM*) serves affordable, creative Chinese
dishes from its location upstairs from the Capital
Yacht Club,

Bars & Nightlife:

For casual fare, flip-flops-and-shorts ambience, live music,
and fun happy hours, choose **Cantina Marina (16)** (*600
Water St. SW, 202-554-8396, www.cantinamarina.com,
summer Su–Th 11:30AM–10PM, F–Sa 11:30AM–11PM,
winter Tu–Sa 11:30AM–10PM*), located right on the dock.
Stop for a pre-theater drink and nibbles at **Next Stage by
José Andrés Catering with Ridgewells (17)** (*1101 Sixth St.
SW, 202-600-4100, www.arenastage.org, open 2½ hours
prior to show*), located on the 3rd floor of the Mead Center

for American Theatre. The **Bar at CityZen
(18)** (*Mandarin Oriental Hotel, 1330
Maryland Ave. SW, 202-787-6006,
www.mandarinoriental.com/washington,
Tu–Th 6PM–11:30PM, F–Sa 5:30PM–
11:30PM*) serves classic cocktails and
champagne drinks. In-the-know diners

find the three-course bar menu a cost-effective way to experience Chef Ziebold's cuisine. Enjoy a signature martini with the upscale crowd at the **Empress Lounge (19)** *(Mandarin Oriental Hotel, 1330 Maryland Ave. SW, 202-787-6006, www.mandarinoriental.com/washington, daily 11:30AM–10:30PM)*. Listen to piano music and jazz on weekend evenings.

WHERE TO SHOP

On the northern end of the promenade, the **Maine Avenue Fish Wharf (20)** *(1100 Maine Ave. SW, daily 8AM–9PM)*, also known as **The Wharf**, is an open-air fish market under the shadow of I-395 where you can get a taste of the old Southwest waterfront. Locals barter for fish, crabs, and lobsters sold from floating barges.

WHERE TO STAY

Check out **Channel Inn (21) ($$)** *(650 Water St., 202-554-2400 or 800-368-5668, www.channelinn.com)*, DC's only waterfront hotel located on a channel of the Potomac River. Comfortable, charmingly decorated rooms all have balconies. Providing well-appointed accommodations, a year-round rooftop pool, a restaurant, lounge, and pub, **L'Enfant Plaza Hotel (22) ($$-$$$)** *(480 L'Enfant Plaza SW, 202-484-1000 or 800-635-5065, www.lenfantplazahotel.com)*, is steps away from the L'Enfant Plaza Metro stop, and a short walk to the Smithsonian museums. For luxury, sophistication, and exceptional dining, choose the **Mandarin Oriental Hotel (23) ($$$)** *(1330 Maryland Ave. SW, 202-554-8588 or*

888-888-1778, *www.mandarinoriental.com/washington).* Enjoy the feng shui-influenced rooms, state-of-the-art fitness center, heated lap pool, and views. **Residence Inn Marriott Washington, DC/Capitol (24) ($$)** *(333 E St. SW, 202-484-8280 or 800-331-3131, www.capitolmarriott. com)* is an all-suite hotel, complete with fully outfitted kitchens, an indoor pool, and complimentary hot breakfast buffet. It's the perfect "home away from home." For good value try the **Capitol Skyline Hotel (25) ($-$$)** *(101 I St. SW, 202-488-7500 or 800-458-7500, www.capitol skyline.com),* offering newly renovated rooms, free Wi-Fi, a competition-sized outdoor swimming pool, and complimentary shuttle service to key sites and Metro stops.

🟢 *to Anacostia*

🔴 *to Deanwood*

• SNAPSHOT •

Anacostia, the district east of the Anacostia River, was one of the first planned suburbs of DC. Reach the neighborhood via Metro's Green Line to the Anacostia stop or drive across the 11th Street Bridge. There are several historic and natural gems in this area, but visitors should take care because it does have a high crime rate. Anacostia is the home of Cedar Hill, the beautifully preserved home of Frederick Douglass, former slave, diplomat, publisher, and presidential advisor. It's also the home of the Smithsonian's Anacostia Museum and Center for African-American History and Culture. Kenilworth Park and Aquatic Gardens is an unexpected oasis filled with lotuses and water lilies. Nationals Park, home of the MLB Washington Nationals, opened in 2008 baseball season. From the stands, fans can watch a game with a view of the Capitol and the Washington Monument in the distance. At the present, there are no hotels or shops to speak of; however, a major revitalization of the area is planned.

PLACES TO SEE
Landmarks:

Take the B2 Metro bus from the Anacostia Metro stop to the **Frederick Douglass National Historic Site (26)** *(1411 W St. SE, 202-426-5961 or 800-967-2283, www. nps.gov/frdo, Apr 16–Oct 15 9AM–5PM, Oct 16–Apr 15 9AM–4:30PM)*. Born a slave, the American abolitionist moved to this handsome Victorian home in 1877; he lived here until his death in 1895. The home, named "Cedar Hill" by Douglass, houses many of his personal possessions: his bowler hat and eyeglasses; a cane owned by Abraham Lincoln (and given to Douglass by Mary

Todd Lincoln); and his personal 1,200 volume library. The Visitor Center offers a 17-minute film about the abolitionist. Ranger-led tours are required to see the home; reservations are encouraged. For a spectacular view of

the city, take the Anacostia Metro or W1 or W2 Metro bus toward Naylor and Good Hope Roads, to **Fort Stanton and Washington Overlook (27)** *(Erie Street near Morris Road; parking lot of Our Lady of Perpetual Help Catholic Church, daily dawn–dusk)*. The fort site is in the woods adjacent to the parking lot; a historic marker stands in the corner of the lot. Situated 380 feet above the Potomac River, this overlook stands adjacent to the original site of Fort Stanton, dating to 1861 as the first of some 60 forts that surrounded the city to protect it from Confederate attacks during the Civil War. Another fort that defended the southern border of the city is

Fort Dupont Park (28) *(Randall Circle SE and Minnesota Ave., 202-426-5961, www.nps.gov/fodu, daily dawn–dusk)*, 376 acres of densely wooded parkland dotted with trails, fields, and basketball courts.

Arts & Entertainment:

The **Anacostia Museum (29)** *(1901 Fort Pl. SE, 202-633-4820, www.anacostia.si.edu, daily 10AM–5PM)*, a branch of the Smithsonian, features a collection of changing exhibits on African-American art, history, and culture. **Anacostia Park (30)** *(entrance to Kenilworth Park recreation area at the westernmost end of Nannie Helen Burroughs Avenue NE, just off I-295 or Kenilworth Avenue, www.nps.gov/nace/anacostia.htm, daily 9:30AM–5:30PM)* covers more than 1,200 acres in Anacostia along the Anacostia River. If you're looking to spot wildlife or play golf—there's the 18-hole Langston Golf Course and a driving range—tennis, or basketball, this is the place. **Kenilworth Park and Aquatic Gardens (31)** *(northeastern section of Anacostia Park, Anacostia Ave. and Douglas St. NE, 202-426-6905, www.nps.gov/keaq, park daily 8AM–dusk, aquatic garden daily 7AM–4PM)* is a little-known natural haven that constitutes about 700 acres and is part of Anacostia Park. It's the only National Park Service site dedicated to showcasing and growing aquatic plants.

chapter 8

VIRGINIA SUBURBS—
ALEXANDRIA, ARLINGTON,
AND BEYOND

MARYLAND SUBURBS—
BETHESDA AND BEYOND

VIRGINIA SUBURBS—
ALEXANDRIA, ARLINGTON,
AND BEYOND

MARYLAND SUBURBS—
BETHESDA AND BEYOND

Places to See:

1. Alexandria
2. Arlington
3. McLean/Great Falls Park
4. Mount Vernon
5. Bethesda
6. National Harbor
7. Glen Echo/Glen Echo Park
8. Potomac/C&O Canal
   National Historic Park
9. Wheaton/Brookside
   Gardens

Note: This map contains bullets only for the town or city where the site is located.

It is sometimes called the City
of Magnificent Distances,
but it might with greater
propriety be termed the City of
Magnificent Intentions…

—*Charles Dickens*

• SNAPSHOT •

The Virginia suburbs of Washington include a diverse

and historic collection of destinations within easy access of downtown DC. Whether you drive or rely on public transportation, you can reach most major landmarks, arts and entertainment spots, eateries, shopping, and hotels in the suburbs within 30 minutes. This section focuses on key places nearby, in Arlington County, Alexandria, and Fairfax County. Arlington is home to a number of important sights, including Arlington National Cemetery and the Marine Corps War Memorial sculpture of

the famous photo of the 1945 flag raising on Iwo Jima. Old Town Alexandria (King Street Metro stops, Blue or Yellow Line) offers antiquing, shopping, historic homes, and more. Is your time limited? Then the must do site is George Washington's home at Mount Vernon in Fairfax County.

●● *to King Street,
or Pentagon City, or Pentagon*

PLACES TO SEE
Landmarks:

Take the King Street Metro stop on the Blue or Yellow Line to reach the heart of Old Town Alexandria, a revitalized colonial town. The two main arteries here are Washington Street, running north and south, and King Street, running east and west, part of a grid that stretches to the Potomac River on the east and to the Braddock Road Metro stop on the northwest. From King Street Metro, walk east along King Street, cross Washington Street, and continue east. Old Town Alexandria is a gem of a place, where history meets the waterfront, and where Scottish roots and small-town, Southern hospitality combine. Wander its cobblestone streets; you'll love its art galleries, gourmet restaurants, home furnishings, antiques shops, and museums. Start at King Street and turn right on South Washington Street; here you'll find some of the Old Town's most appealing historic places. Stop first at **The Lyceum** *(201 S. Washington St., corner of Prince St., 703-838-4994, http://alexandriava.gov/lyceum, M–Sa 10AM–5PM, Su 1PM–5PM)*. Housed in a superb two-story 1839 Greek Revival

193

structure, it presents the city's history through documents, photographs, furniture, decorative arts, tools, and Civil War artifacts. Return to King Street and walk east toward the river to **Gadsby's Tavern Museum** *(134 N. Royal St., 703-746-4242, http://alexandriava.gov/gadsbystavern, Apr–Oct Tu–Sa 10AM–5PM, Su–M 1PM–5PM, Nov–Mar W–Sa 11AM–4PM, Su 1PM–4PM)*. George Washington and Thomas Jefferson, among other early American notables, were guests at this restored 18th-century hotel and tavern. **Market Square** *(301 King St.)* hosts a **Farmers' Market** *(301 King St., www.alexandriava.gov/farmersmarket, Sa 5:30AM–11AM)* thought to be among the nation's oldest, offering fresh veggies, fruits, honey, baked goods, plants, quilts, and more. **Carlyle House** *(121 N. Fairfax St., 703-549-2997, www.carlylehouse.org, Tu–Sa 10AM–4PM, Su noon–4PM)*, a block away, is a Georgian Palladian manor household dating to 1753, built by city founder John Carlyle, a Scottish merchant. This was where General Edward Braddock planned strategies for the French and Indian War. If you need help with your stay in Alexandria, stop at **Ramsay House**, Alexandria's oldest house and its modern-day visitors' center *(221 King St., 703-838-5005 or 800-388-9119, www.visitalexandria.com, daily 9AM–8PM)*. Another historic place is the **Stabler-Leadbeater Apothecary Museum** *(105–107 S. Fairfax St., 703-838-3852, http://oha.alexandriava.gov/apothecary, Apr–Oct Su–M 1PM–5PM, Tu–Sa 10AM–5PM; Nov–Mar W–Sa 11AM–4PM, Su 1PM–4PM)*. Quaker Edward Stabler began his family pharmacy here in 1792. Most of the furnishings, herbs, and potions remain intact. Famous patrons included George and Martha Washington and Robert E. Lee.

Arts & Entertainment:

At the foot of King Street in Alexandria is the **Torpedo Factory Art Center** *(105 N. Union St., 703-838-4565, www.torpedofactory.org, daily 10AM–6PM, Th till 9PM)*. This former U.S. Navy torpedo plant houses the studios and workshops of over 160 painters, potters, sculptors, and other artisans. Most of the arts and crafts are for sale. It's also home to the **Art League School** *(gallery hours: M–W 10AM–6PM, Th 10AM–9PM, F–Sa 10AM–6PM, Su noon–6PM)*, which hosts artist exhibits that are open to the public, and the **Alexandria Archaeology Museum** *(www.alexandriaarchaeology.org, Tu–F 10AM–3PM, Sa 10AM–5PM, Su 1PM–5PM)*. The **Little Theatre of Alexandria** *(600 Wolfe St., 703-683-0496, www.thelittle theatre.com, box office Tu–F 1PM–9PM, weekend hours during performance dates, Sa–Su 1PM–4PM, 7PM–9PM, Su 1PM–4PM)*, the oldest award-winning community theater group in the DC area, boasts a seven-show season. The **Old Town Theater** *(815-1/2 King St., 703-683-8888, http://tickets.oldtowntheater.com)*, built in 1914, shows first-rate films on two screens. Said to be one of the best places outside the Blue Ridge Mountains to hear bluegrass music, the **Birchmere Music Hall** *(3701 Mount Vernon Ave., 703-549-7500, www.birchmere.com, box office 5PM–9PM on performance nights)* draws crowds with concerts featuring top names in country, folk, blues, and alternative music.

PLACES TO EAT AND DRINK

Eateries of every kind line the streets of Old Town Alexandria *(King Street Metro stop, Blue or Yellow Line)*. At the foot of King Street near the water, you'll find **The Fish Market ($-$$)** *(105 King St., 703-836-5676, www.fishmarketoldtown.com, daily 11:30AM–11:30PM)*, located in a 200-year-old historic building, and known for its clam chowder, oysters, crab cakes, and lively crowd. Nearby is the **Chart House ($$-$$$)** *(1 Cameron St., 703-684-5080, www.chart-house.com, M–Th 11:30AM–3PM, 4PM–10PM, F–Sa 11:30AM–3PM, 4PM–11PM, Su 11AM–10PM)*, part of a national chain. It offers seafood, steak, and great views of the Potomac River. Signature dishes include snapper Hemingway and hot chocolate lava cake. For fabulous new American, it's **Restaurant Eve ($$$)** *(110 South Pitt St., 703-706-0450, www.restauranteve.com, M–Th 11:30AM–11:30PM, F 11:30AM–12:30AM, Sa 5:50PM–11:30PM)*. Dinner reservations are hard to come by, but you can pop in for the two-course lunch menu at the lounge to say that you've been. Just a few doors down, the inviting **Union Street Public House ($$)** *(121 S. Union St., 703-548-1785, www.unionpublichouse.com, M–F 11:30AM–10PM, Sa 11:30AM–11PM, Su 11AM–10PM)* treats you to Southern specialties in tavern-style surrounds. Prefer Italian? The stone and mahogany dining room at **Landini Brothers ($$-$$$)** *(115 King St., 703-836-8404, www.landini brothers.com, M–Sa 11:30AM–11PM, Su 11:30AM–10PM)* is the perfect setting for traditional Tuscan fare. **The Wharf ($-$$$)** *(119 King St., 703-836-2836, www. wharfrestaurant.com, M–Th 11AM–10:30PM, F–Sa 11AM–*

11PM, Su 11AM–10PM) features 1790s architecture, with beams charred during the Civil War. The menu combines seasonal Chesapeake favorites with contemporary dishes. **Il Porto Ristorante ($$)** *(121 King St., corner of Lee St., 703-836-8833, www.ilportoristorante.com, F–Sa 11AM–11PM, Su 11AM–10PM)* serves fine Italian cuisine in a cozy dining room in the heart of Old Town Alexandria. Enjoy steak and seafood in casual yet elegant environs at **The Warehouse Bar & Grill ($$)** *(214 King St., 703-683-6868, www.warehousebarandgrill.com, M–Th 11AM–10:30PM, F 11AM–11PM, Sa 8:30AM–11PM, Su 10AM–9:30PM)*. The decor of this historic building includes caricatures of the local gentry. Have a drink at the antique

mahogany bar. At the other end of King Street, closer to the Metro, is **Las Tapas Restaurant ($-$$$)** *(710 King St., 703-836-4000, www.lastapas.us, M–Tu 4PM–10PM, W 11:30AM–10PM, Th 11:30AM–11PM, F 11:30AM–1AM, Sa 10AM–1AM, Su 10AM–10PM)*, featuring over 62 varieties of tapas, wines and sherries from Spain, plus flamenco dancers and Spanish guitar music. The sophisticated **Morrison House Grille ($$-$$$)** *(Morrison House Hotel, 116 S. Alfred St., 703-838-8000 or 866-834-6628, www.morrisonhouse.com, M–Th 7AM–10AM, 6PM–9PM, F 7AM–10AM, 6PM–10PM, Sa 8AM–10AM, tea 2PM–5PM, 6PM–10PM, Su 8AM–10AM, 11AM–2PM, 6PM–9PM)* serves an American menu centered around meat, fish, and locally-grown produce. The warm and friendly **Taverna Cretekou ($-$$)** *(818 King St., 703-548-8688,* *www.tavernacretekou.com, Tu–F 11:30AM–2:30PM, 5PM–10PM, Sa noon–10:30PM, Su 11AM–3PM, 5PM–9:30PM)* serves authentic Mediterranean specialties in a setting reminiscent of the Greek Isles. For Texas, Cincinnati, or vegetarian chili, try the original **Hard Times Café ($)** *(1404 King St., 703-837-0050, www.hardtimes.com, M–F 11AM–10PM, F–Sa 11AM–midnight)*, and enjoy its country-western jukebox with your beer. One of the most romantic restaurants in the area is located north of Old Town on the Potomac River. **Indigo Landing ($$)** *(Washington Sailing Marina, George Washington Pky., 703-548-0001, www.indigolanding.com, M–Sa 11:30AM–9PM, Su 10AM–9PM)* offers contemporary, low-country cuisine in a setting overlooking the Washington Sailing Marina. Try the jumbo lump blue crab cakes with sweet potato puree or their signature scampi.

WHERE TO SHOP

Can't resist decorative arts, antiques, clothing boutiques, and gift emporiums? Old Town Alexandria *(King Street Metro stop, Blue or Yellow Line)* is for you. Toward the foot of King Street, you'll find **Hysteria** *(125 South Fairfax St., 703-548-1615, M–Sa 11AM–6PM, Su noon–6PM)*, which stocks a smart mix of classics like Tory Burch and Trina Turk and hip designs from Jodi Arnold and Leona. **The Virginia Shop** *(104 S. Union St., 703-836-3160 or 888-297-8288, www.thevirginiashop. com, M–Th 10AM–8PM, F–Sa 10AM–9PM, Su noon–6PM)*, a cornucopia of traditional decorative arts and accessories, Virginia wines, fudge, peanuts, biscuit mixes, and other souvenirs displayed in a two-story 1765 structure. **Why Not?** (*200 King St., 703-548-4420, M–Th 10AM–5:30PM, F–Sa 10AM–6PM, Su noon–5PM*), with its toys, books, games, and clothes, is a fun place to shop with or without kids. If you can't get enough of Christmas ornaments, head around the corner to **The Christmas Attic** (*125 Union St., 703-548-2829 or 800-881-0084, www.christmas attic.com, M 10AM–7PM, T–W 10AM–5PM, Th–Sa 10AM–7PM, Su 11AM–6PM*), featuring Christopher Radko ornaments, Byers figurines, and patriotic gift items, too. Closer to the King Street Metro stop, the **Crate and Barrel Outlet** (*1700 Prince St., 703-739-8800, www.crateand barrel.com, M–Sa 10AM–7PM, Su noon–5PM*) offers its home designs discounted up to 70 percent. **Artfully Chocolate Kingsbury Confections** (*2003A Mt. Vernon Ave., 703-635-7917, www.thecocoagallery.com, Su–M 11AM– 8:30PM, Tu–W 11AM–8PM, Th 11AM–9PM, F 11AM–10PM, Sa 10AM–10PM*) tempts with unique confections like chipotle-cinnamon truffles and Turkish apricots dipped in dark chocolate. You must try the café's hot chocolate. Choose from a dozen different varieties, including the "Liz Taylor," a semisweet hot chocolate infused with lavender. Can't decide? Go for the sampler and you enjoy three different types. The fair trade chain **Ten Thousand Villages** (*915 King St., 703-684-1435, www.alexandria.tenthousand villages.com, M–Sa 11AM–7PM, Su noon–6PM*) specializes in handicrafts; folk art, home decor, and more by international artisans. **Tradition de France** (*1113 King St., 703-836-5340, www.traditiondefrance.com, M 10AM–6PM, W–Sa 10AM–6PM, Su noon–6PM*) features three floors of handmade imported French furniture, including armoires, leather couches, and tables with inlaid patterns and marble inserts. **Random Harvest** *(810 King St., 703-548-8820, www.randomharvesthome.com, M–Sa 11AM–6PM, Su noon–6PM)* offers an assortment of antiques, new furniture, and accessories.

WHERE TO STAY

The Old Town's **Morrison House ($$$)** *(116 S. Alfred St., 703-838-8000 or 866-834-6628, www.morrisonhouse.com)* is an elegant colonial-style inn with four-poster beds, intimate public rooms, fireplaces, and an acclaimed restaurant. It's ten blocks from the King Street Metro. **Hotel Monaco ($$-$$$)** *(480 King St., 703-549-6080 or 800-368-5047, www.monaco-alexandria.com)* is the only hotel in the historic district. This posh boutique hotel is noted for its royal treatment of pets; from April–October, there are doggie happy hours each week on Tuesday and Thursday evenings. For value and a welcoming atmosphere at the north end of Old Town, book **Best Western Old Colony Inn ($-$$)** *(1101 N. Washington St., 703-739-2222 or 800-528-1234, www.hotel-alexandria.com)*. A hot breakfast buffet is included, and the hotel offers a business center, fitness center, Internet access, a complimentary snack kitchen, plus a free shuttle to the center of Old Town.

● ● *to Rosslyn*

● *to Arlington Cemetery*

● ● *to Pentagon, or Pentagon City*

● *to Clarendon, or Ballston-MU*

PLACES TO SEE
Landmarks:

To organize your visit and find brochures and bus sched-ules, stop at the **Arlington Visitors Center** *(1301 S. Joyce St., 800-677-6267, Pentagon City Metro stop, Blue or Yellow Line, www.stayarlington.com, daily 9AM–5PM).* There are exhibits and a multimedia film here, as well. You can then walk to the **Marine Corps War Memorial**, commonly known as the **Iwo Jima Memorial** *(exit the Metro, turn right on Moore Street, go to end of block and turn left, go 1/2 block to Lynn Street, cross Lynn and turn right, follow the sidewalk*

along the Route 50 overpass to the memorial on the left, 703-289-2500, www.nps.gov/gwmp/usmc.htm). The largest cast bronze statue in the world, it re-creates the raising of the American flag on Mount Suribachi during World War II, and is dedicated to all Marines who have died in battle since 1775. From the surrounding park you'll enjoy breathtaking views of the Washington Monument, the Lincoln Memorial, and the Capitol. If you're in Washington for Independence Day, it's an ideal place from which to watch the fireworks display. Within the same park is the 127-foot-tall **Netherlands Carillon** *(next to the Iwo Jima Memorial, 703-289-2500, www.nps.gov/gwmp/carillon.htm)*, a 50-bell tower the Dutch people gave to the U.S. in gratitude for its aid during and after World War II. The carillon plays "Westminster Chimes" each hour and Armed Forces anthems, U.S. and Netherlands anthems, and other selections at noon and 6PM. The park service Web site lists the full program schedule. From the Arlington Cemetery Metro stop on the Blue Line, visit **Arlington National Cemetery** *(Memorial Dr. and Jefferson Davis Hwy., 703-607-8000, www.arlingtoncemetery.org/index.htm, Apr–Sep 8AM–7PM; Oct–Mar 8AM–5PM)*, a national shrine to over

a quarter of a million men and women who have died defending the U.S., from Revolutionary soldiers to Operation Iraqi Freedom, as well as veterans and former slaves. The cemetery's visitor center is located about a block from the cemetery, where you can purchase tickets for the narrated **"Tourmobile"** *(202-554-5100, www.tourmobile.com)* shuttle bus, which will drive you through the cemetery. You'll want to see the Tomb of the Unknowns, where soldiers from World Wars I and II and the Korean War are buried. Time your visit to see the changing of the guard in front of these tombs *(Apr–Sept semi-hourly 8AM–7PM, Oct–Mar hourly 8AM–5PM)*. John F. Kennedy is buried here, along with his wife, Jacqueline, and his brothers Robert and Ted. Kennedy's grave is marked with an eternal flame. The grounds of **Arlington House/The Robert E. Lee Memorial** *(Arlington National Cemetery, 703-235-1530, www.nps.gov/arho, daily 9:30AM–4:30PM)* offer spectacular views of DC. This is the former home of George Washington's adopted grandson, George Washington Parke Custis, whose daughter, Mary Anna Randolph, married Robert E. Lee. It was here that Lee resigned his commission in the U.S. Army to fight for the South. The federal government confiscated the property and designated a 200-acre section as a military cemetery. To the southeast, **The Pentagon**, spread over 34 acres *(the Pentagon Metro stop on the Blue or Yellow Line; tours M–F 9AM–3PM, request online or through your state representative at least two weeks in advance; 703-614-1642, http://pentagon.afis.osd.mil/tours.cfm)*, is headquarters of the Department of Defense. It's one of the world's largest office buildings (three times the floor space of the Empire State Building), with over 17 miles of corridor, yet it takes only seven minutes to walk between any two points in the building. A 90 acre preserve in the middle of the Potomac, **Theodore Roosevelt Island Memorial Park** *(Metro stop Rosslyn, walk 2 blocks to cross the footbridge, www.nps.gov/this, daily 6AM–10PM)* is a naturalist's delight with several marked flat walking trails through forests and marshland. There is also a memorial plaza dedicated to Roosevelt here with a statue and four granite slabs etched with some of his (prophetic) words on conservation.

Arts & Entertainment:

Take the Metro to Pentagon City on the Blue or Yellow Line to the **Drug Enforcement Administration Museum and Visitors Center** *(700 Army Navy Dr., Pentagon City, 202-307-3463, www.deamuseum.org, Tu–F 10AM–4PM)*; here you'll learn how the illicit drug industry has affected American society and how federal law enforcement tries to control these substances through "Illegal Drugs in America: A Modern History," the permanent exhibition.

PLACES TO EAT & DRINK

For that classic American chili, it's hard to beat the **Hard Times Café ($)** *(3028 Wilson Blvd., 703-528-2233, Clarendon Metro stop, Orange Line, www.hardtimes.com, Su–Th 11AM–1AM, F–Sa 11AM–3AM)* chain of eateries. Try its "Chili Bubba," cornbread topped with chili, cheddar cheese, tomatoes, onions, and sour cream. Craving kabob? Visit **Kabob Bazaar ($)** *(3133 Wilson Blvd., 703-522-8999, Clarendon Metro stop, Orange Line, www.kabobbazaar.com, M–Th 11AM–10PM, F–Sa 11AM–11PM, Su noon–10PM)*. Get the saffron-marinated lemon chicken. Amazing. Prefer Tex-Mex? Choose **Uncle Julio's ($)** *(4301 N. Fairfax Drive, 703-528-3131, Ballston-MU Metro stop, Orange Line, www.unclejulios.com, Su–Th 11AM–10:30PM, F–Sa 11AM–11:30PM)* for fajitas, margaritas, and a festive atmosphere. For Memphis barbecue and rhythm and blues, try **Red Hot & Blue BBQ ($)** *(1600 Wilson Blvd., 703-276-7427, Rosslyn Metro stop, Blue or Orange Line, www.redhotandblue.com, Su–Th*

11AM–10PM, F–Sa till 11PM), serving plentiful portions with friendly service. Get your pho fix at **Pho 75 ($)** *(1721 Wilson Blvd., 703-525-7355, Rosslyn Metro stop, Blue or Orange Line, daily 11AM–8PM)*. A hot bowl of noodles in broth with a side plate of bean sprouts, basil, and lime is a satisfying and healthy "cheap eat." For creative French- and Italian- inspired fare in relaxed surroundings, choose **Bistro Bistro ($-$$)** *(4021 S. 28th St., The Village at Shirlington, off I-395, 703-379-0300, www.bistro-bistro. com, M–Th 11:30AM–10PM, F–Sa 11:30AM–11PM, Su 10AM–10PM)*. For 10-ounce burgers that some say are the best in DC, stop in at **Ray's Hell Burger** *(1713 Wilson Blvd., 703-841-0001, M–Th, Sa–Su 11AM–10PM, F 11AM–11PM)*. You might even spot President Obama eating there!

WHERE TO SHOP

The Fashion Centre at Pentagon City *(1100 S. Hayes St., 703-415-2400, Pentagon City Metro stop, Blue or Yellow Line, www.simon.com, M–Sa 10AM–9:30PM, Su 11AM–6PM)* ranks as one of the most popular malls in the region. Convenient to downtown, it draws crowds to its 170 stores, food court, full-service restaurants, and Ritz-Carlton Hotel. A glass-enclosed, skylit, multilevel shopping hub, its stores range from Macy's and Nordstrom to L'Occitane, MAC  Cosmetics, and Apple. Nearby **Pentagon Row** *(1101 S. Joyce St., Pentagon City Metro stop, Blue or Yellow Line, www.pentagonrow.com, M–Sa 10AM–9PM, Su noon–6PM)* is a chic outdoor shopping center which features specialty retailers, cafés, a gym, Starbucks, an Irish pub, and an in-season ice-skating rink. For a small-town feel not far from downtown Washington, try **The Village at Shirlington** (*2700 S. Quincy St., off I-395, the Shirley Highway, accessible by car, www.villageatshirlington. com*), another outdoor mall, for varied shops, restaurants, and movie theaters.

WHERE TO STAY

The Ritz-Carlton at Pentagon City ($$$) (*1250 S. Hayes St., 703-415-5000 or 800-241-3333, www.ritzcarlton.com, Pentagon City Metro stop, Blue or Yellow Line*) pampers guests with featherbeds, marble baths, an indoor pool, a fitness center, and the convenience of the Metro at your front door. **The Virginian Suites ($-$$)** (*1500 Arlington Blvd., 703-522-9600 or 800-275-2866, www.virginian suites.com, Rosslyn Metro stop, Blue or Orange Line*) is family- and budget-friendly, with an outdoor pool and sundeck, complimentary coffee, newspapers, shuttle to the Metro, and a local grocery store. Studio-style and one-bedroom suites have fully equipped kitchens.

*Take Route 193, Exit 44 from the Beltway,
then go 4.5 miles west*

One of the most dramatic places in the Virginian suburbs is **Great Falls Park** *(Great Falls National Park, 9200 Old Dominion Drive, www.nps.gov/grfa, daily 7AM–dusk)*, where spectacular waterfalls tumble 76 feet over jagged rocks in the Potomac River. Located 14 miles up the George Washington Memorial Parkway from Washington, DC, this 800-acre park is great for relaxation or hiking.

Nearby dining includes **Kazan ($$)** *(6813 Redmond Dr., 703-734-1960, www.kazanrestaurant.com, M–Th 11:30AM–2:30PM, 5:30PM–10PM, F 11:30AM–2:30PM, 5:30PM–10:30PM, Sa 5:30PM–10:30PM)*, offering Turkish food and music.

Area shopping centers include **Tysons Galleria** *(2001 International Dr., 703-827-7700, www.tysonsgalleria.com, M–Sa 10AM–9PM, Su noon–6PM)*, with Burberry, Anthropologie, and Coach, among others. Another option is the huge **Tysons Corner Center** *(1961 Chain Bridge Rd., 703-847-7300, www.shoptysons.com, M–Sa 10AM–9:30PM, Su 11AM–7PM)*, with stores in every category, from clothes to eyewear to jewelery to stationery.

Out this way the **Westin Reston Heights** *(11750 Sunrise Valley Dr., Reston, 703-391-9000, www.westonreston.com)*

is contemporary and stylish, with well-appointed rooms and excellent **Vinifera Bistro and Wine Bar** on-site, all conveniently located midway between DC and the Dulles airport.

MOUNT VERNON (4), VIRGINIA

Southern end of the George Washington Memorial Parkway, 703-780-2000, www.mountvernon.org; use Metro's Huntington stop on the Yellow Line, go to lower level for Fairfax Connector Bus 101, 703-339-7200; 20-minute ride to the estate, or see chapter 7, **Spirit Cruises (8)**, *p. 182.*

Don't miss **Mount Vernon Estate and Gardens** *(www.mountvernon.org, Apr–Aug 8AM–5PM, Sep, Oct, Mar 9AM–5PM, Nov–Feb 9AM–4PM),* located several miles south of Old Town Alexandria and just sixteen miles south of DC. This was the home of George and

Martha Washington from 1759 until 1799. Tour the mansion, outbuildings, and the four-acre working pioneer farmer site. At the state-of-the-art Ford Orientation Center, don't miss the film *We Fight to be Free,* which shares a wealth of information

about Washington's life, including his teenage years, military career, and presidency. Plan to spend several hours here in order to tour the mansion and roam Mt. Vernon's magnificent grounds.

MARYLAND SUBURBS—
BETHESDA AND BEYOND

● SNAPSHOT ●

Maryland's suburbs are a collection of cities, towns, and districts that create an often-welcome change of pace from the DC dither. The area—largely Montgomery County, Maryland—includes public gardens, ethnic dining, art galleries, boutiques, entertainment choices, preserved farmland, parkland, and historic sites. In addition, it is home to the National Institutes of Health, the National Library of Medicine, and the National Naval Medical Center. Here, we focus on the best of Bethesda, with highlights from other communities.

PLACES TO SEE
Arts & Entertainment:

The Maryland suburbs have a variety of musical, theatrical, and dance programs. **Strathmore Hall Arts Center** *(10701 Rockville Pike, 301-530-5889, www.strathmore. org, box office M, Tu, Th, F 10AM– 5PM, W 10AM–9PM, Sa 10AM–2PM)* is a focal point for arts in the area, including art exhibitions, literary lectures, chamber music, folk music, jazz concert series, afternoon musical teas, performances for children, and outdoor concerts. Strathmore is also the second year-round venue of the **Baltimore Symphony Orchestra**. All programs are set in the Georgian-style mansion or in a 2,000-seat concert hall in the Music Center. Attend a performance at **Imagination Stage** *(4908 Auburn Ave., 301-280-1660, www.imaginationstage.org, box office daily 10AM–5PM)*, the largest multidisciplinary theater organization for young people in the Washington DC area. Literary adaptations, world premieres, and classic plays are featured.

PLACES TO EAT AND DRINK

Bethesda is a fun place to search for eateries. If you take the Red Line to the Bethesda Metro stop, you'll be able to walk to most places easily. One of the closest is the

Daily Grill ($$) *(One Bethesda Metro Center, 301-656-6100, www.dailygrill.com, M–Th 6:30AM–11PM, F–Sa 6:30AM–midnight, Su 6:30AM–10PM)*, serving traditional grill favorites. Family-friendly **Moongate ($)** *(4613 Willow Ln., 301-657-3740, Su–Th 11AM–10PM, F–Sa 11AM–11PM)* offers Chinese food as good as the portions are plentiful. For hot and cold sandwiches, salads, and sides, try popular **Booeymonger Bethesda ($)** *(4600 East West Highway, 301-718-9550, www.booeymonger.com,*

M–F 7:30AM–10PM, Sa 8AM–5PM, Su 8AM–4PM). **Persimmon ($$)** *(7003 Wisconsin Ave., 301-654-9860, www.persimmon.com, M–F 11:30AM–9PM, Sa 5PM–10PM, Su 11AM–9PM)* is Bethesda's splashy high-ender. Don't miss the pecan-crusted rack of lamb. For tasty Northern Indian food, go to **Delhi Dhaba Punjabi Grill ($)** *(7236 Woodmont Ave., 301-718-0008, www.delhidhaba.com, M–F 11:30AM–3PM, 5PM–10PM, Sa 11:30AM–10:30PM, Su 11:30AM–10PM)*. Every neighborhood should have a spot like **Black's Bar & Kitchen ($$)** *(7750 Woodmont Ave., 301-652-5525, www.blacksbarandkitchen.com, M–Th 11:30AM–10PM, F 11:30AM–11PM, Sa noon–midnight, Su 11AM–10PM)*. The new American menu excels with its raw bar choices. **Café Deluxe ($)** *(4910 Elm St., 301-656-3131, www.cafedeluxe.com, M–Th 11:30AM–10:30PM, F–Sa 11:30AM–11PM, Su 10:30AM–10PM)* dishes up comfort foods like grilled meat loaf as well as innovative

selections. **BGR-The Burger Joint** (*4827 Fairmont Ave., 301-358-6137, www.burgerjointdc.com, Su–Th 11AM–9PM, F–Sa 11AM–10PM*) is known for its made-to-order burgers, prepared with quality beef and fresh ingredients. Add fries and a shake and enjoy!

WHERE TO SHOP

Art collectors will find galleries galore in downtown Bethesda. **Waverly St. Gallery** (*4600 East-West Highway, 301-951-9441, www.waverlystreetgallery.com, Tu–Sa noon–6PM*) connects rising artists with new collectors. **Fraser Gallery** (*7700 Wisconsin Ave., Suite E, 301-718-9651, www.thefrasergallery.com, Tu–Sa 11:30AM–6PM*) was founded by award-winning photographer Catriona Fraser, who personally selects the artists exhibited here. **Gallery St. Elmo** (*4938 St. Elmo Ave., 301-654-0576, www.gallerystelmo.com, M noon–5PM, Tu–W 11AM–6PM, Th 11AM–7PM, F–Sa 11AM–6PM*) is a consignment shop offering furniture, vintage jewelry, and decorative accessories. Take a primping break at **Blue Mercury** (*7105 Bethesda Lane, 301-986-0070, www.bluemercury.com, M–Sa 10AM–8PM, Su noon–6PM*). The DC area-based beauty chain is the place for hard-to-find beauty and body products and a spa that offers quick-stop or day-long indulgences. If you're looking for trendy women's sportswear, shoes, or accessories, shop at **Luna** (*7232 Woodmont Ave., 301-656-1111, www.shopluna.com, M–Sa 10AM–7PM, Su noon–5PM*). **White Flint Mall** (*11301 Rockville Pike, 301-231-7467, White Flint Metro stop, Red Line, www.shopwhiteflint.com, M–Sa 10AM–9:30PM, Su* *noon–6PM)* has one of the best concentrations of upscale stores in one place, just a block away from the White Flint Metro station.

WHERE TO STAY

Prefer to stay far from the madding crowd? The **Doubletree Hotel-Bethesda ($$)** *(8120 Wisconsin Ave., 301-652-2000 or 800-955-7359, http://doubletree. hilton.com)* fills the bill with thoughtfully appointed rooms, a fitness area, and pool. The Great Room, the hotel's gathering space, is open for breakfast, lunch, and dinner. The **Bethesda Marriott ($$)** *(5151 Pooks Hill Rd., 301-897-9400, http://marriott.com)* has 407 rooms, an indoor and outdoor pool, exercise equipment, and onsite restaurants.

● *Take I-295, I-95 or I-495*

Fronting the Potomac River and just 12 miles south of downtown DC, **National Harbor** *(www.nationalharbor.com)* is a 350-acre retail, dining, and entertainment destination complex. The area is still in transition, but you will find a marina, hotels, scores of galleries, stores, and restaurants. Lots of activities center around National Harbor's marina. You can rent canoes and kayaks from **Calleva** *(160 National Plaza, www.calleva.org)* or go on a narrated Potomac River cruise with the **Potomac Riverboat Company** *(137 National Harbor, 703-684-0580, www.potomacriverboatco.com)*. Afterward, stroll along the promenade to take in the water views and gawk at the docked pleasure crafts. At the Plaza, you can't miss "The Awakening," a 100-foot sculpture of a giant struggling to free himself from the sand. The Plaza is also the site for free concerts, street performances, and special events. Families with tots will want to check out **Launch Zone** *(112 Waterfront St., 301-686-0225, Apr–May M–Sa 10AM–5PM, Su 11AM–5PM, June–Sept 6 M–Th 10AM–5PM, F–Sa 10AM–7PM, Su 11AM–5PM, Sept 7–Oct M–Sa 10AM–5PM, Su 11AM–5PM, Nov–Mar M–F 10AM–3PM, Sa 10AM–5PM, Su 11AM–5PM)*, a play space that serves as a preview of the exhibits of the **National Children's Museum** *(www.ncm.museum)*, which is set to open a brand-new facility here in 2013. Along the waterfront, there are shops

215

galore. Head to **South Moon Under** *(100 American Way, 301-567-0511, M–Th 10AM–7PM, F–Sa 10AM–9PM, Su 11AM–6PM, www.southmoonunder.com)* for trendy women's wear, **Artcraft** *(140 American Way, 301-567-6616, www.artcraftonline.com, M–Sa 9AM–10PM, Su 11AM–5PM)* for whimsical gifts, and **Tiki and Me** *(141 Waterfront St., 301-839-3911, www.tikiandme.com, M–Th 10AM–7PM, F–Sa 10AM–9PM, Su 11AM–6PM)* for pet apparel and playthings. For dining, take your pick of high-end restaurants like New York steakhouse **Bond 45 ($$$)** *(149 Waterfront St., 301-839-1445, www.bond45.com, M–Th 5PM–10PM, F 5PM–11PM, Sa noon–11PM, Su noon–10PM)* and Asian fusion delight **Grace's Mandarin ($$)** *(188 Waterfront St., 301-839-3788, www.gracesrestaurants.com, M–Th 11:30AM–11PM, Sa 11:30AM–midnight, Su 11:30AM–10PM)*. Or grab a bite at casual eateries like **Baja Fresh ($)** *(186 Waterfront St., 301-839-1377, www.bajafresh.com)* or **Cakelove ($)** *(160 National Plaza, 301-686-0340, www.cakelove.com, Su–Th 11:30AM–7:30PM, F–Sa 11AM–9PM)*. Stay the night at the **Gaylord National Resort and Convention Center** *(201 Water St., 301-965-2000, www.gaylordhotels.com)*—it's an attraction in its own right. The luxurious hotel boasts 2,000 rooms with plentiful amenities, grand public spaces, an 18-story atrium, an indoor/outdoor pool, a full-service spa, and several restaurants and bars. You won't ever have to leave.

GLEN ECHO (7), MARYLAND

🔴 *to Friendship Heights or Bethesda;
take Montgomery County Ride-on bus #29*

Glen Echo Park *(7300 MacArthur Blvd., 301-634-2222, www.glenechopark.org, daily dawn–dusk)* is a family-oriented, historic outdoor spot. Ride a restored 1921 Dentzel Carousel. Enjoy a puppet show or a theatrical performance at Adventure Theatre. There are also art galleries, and big-band and ball-room dancing on weekends in the 1933 Spanish ballroom. The **Discovery Creek Children's Museum** in the park is located in a one-room schoolhouse and features innovative educational programs and exhibits focusing on the environment.

The **Clara Barton National Historic Site** *(5801 Oxford Rd., 301-320-1410, www.nps.gov/clba, daily 10AM–5PM, tours on the hour, last tour at 4PM)*, housed in a yellow ware-house-like building, was originally used as a storehouse for the American Red Cross in 1891. In 1897 the structure was remodeled when Clara Barton moved there, and her furnishings and personal effects are still on display.

By car take MacArthur Blvd. from DC to the end

One of the most beautiful places in Montgomery County is the **C&O Canal National Historic Park** *(11710 MacArthur Blvd., 301-767-3714, www.nps.gov/grfa, daily dawn–dusk, Visitor Center daily 9AM–4:30PM)*, which offers scenic views

of the **Great Falls** in Virginia. The National Park Service, which operates the park and the **Great Falls Tavern Visitor Center**, offers canal boat rides and interpretive programs. Enjoy a picnic as you hike the various trails through the forest and along the river. Rock climbing and kayaking are also available for the very experienced. Arguably the prettiest restaurant in the Maryland suburbs is **Normandie Farm ($$)** *(10710 Falls Rd., 301-983-8838, www.normandiefarm.com, Tu–Sa 11:30AM–2PM, 5:30PM–10PM, Su 11AM–2PM, 5PM–9PM)*, where every meal is a special event. Combining a country atmosphere with French/continental cuisine, this antique-bedecked dining spot serves its now-famous popovers and raspberry preserves with every meal. Order the blackened stuffed filet of salmon, or beef Wellington. Its **Margery's Lounge**, adjacent to the lobby, provides live music on Friday and Saturday evenings. During warm weather, try the outdoor café.

● *to Wheaton*

Got a green thumb? Plan a trip to **Brookside Gardens** *(Wheaton Regional Park, 1800 Glenallan Ave., 301-962-1400, www.montgomeryparks.org/brookside, daily dawn–dusk, Visitors Center daily 9AM–5PM, Conservatories daily 10AM–5PM)*, a 50-acre botanical oasis located within **Wheaton Regional Park**, with an azalea garden, a rose garden, a fragrance garden, a children's garden, a Japanese-style garden, and a trial garden. The garden also houses two conservatories of tropical plants. In addition, there is a horticultural reference library and adult and children's programs.

230

NOTES

NOTES

NOTES